Contents

Acknowledgements

The third edition of *The Teaching of History in Primary Schools* depended, even more than previous editions, on the contributions of student teachers and their tutors working on Initial Teacher Training courses and teachers and children in partnership schools. Thanks are especially due to those students whose empirical studies in history are quoted in Chapters 2 and 3; previous pupils and teachers of Greenvale School, Croydon, whose work is cited in Chapters 4 and 6; pupils and teachers at Stramongate School, Kendal, who contributed to case studies in Chapters 3 and 5; colleagues at St Martin's College who explored links between history and their own subject specialisms: Robin Foster in mathematics, Sam Twiselton in English, Kevin Hamel in music and ICT, and to Rob David for the very helpful list of history web sites referred to in Chapter 5.

The support of colleagues at St Martin's library Ambleside, and in particular of Philippa Hope, whose understanding of both children's literature and of history contributed to the success of the case studies in Chapter 5, is also much appreciated; a true 'librarian's librarian'.

Introduction

Here is a new edition of *The Teaching of History in Primary Schools* for the new millennium! The first edition (published in 1992 as *The Teaching of History*) celebrated the entitlement of all primary school children, for the first time, to learn history as part of a broad and rich curriculum and to engage with genuine historical enquiry from their earliest years. It aimed to show primary school teachers, in basic practical ways, how the National Curriculum for History, introduced in 1991, could be implemented.

The second edition (1995) honoured the amazing sea change that teachers had brought about in the teaching of history during those few intervening years, through being adventurous and resilient in trying out new ideas, drawing on the wealth of new resources which followed in the wake of the National Curriculum. This seemed to have established a secure and valued place for history in primary education.

In schools all over the country could be found school museums, displays of 'old things', presentations of local and family history investigations, pictures and models recording visits to sites, museums, galleries and Living History Reconstructions. These were often projects which teachers, particularly at Key Stage 1, had initially embarked upon reluctantly but subsequently discovered how enjoyable and appropriate they could be. Gradually teachers took history into account in curriculum and classroom organisation and management, and related it to their existing understanding of how children learn.

The then newly secure position of primary history meant that teachers were able, for the first time, to draw on a variety of sources of support. There was a massive response from publishers who competed energetically to produce materials of all kinds to support the teaching of history in the primary school. Books, posters, slides, replica sources, audio and video tapes, were designed to develop progression in children's historical thinking. Organisations such as English Heritage, the National Trust and museum education departments developed a wealth of materials, suggestions and experiences linked to the National Curriculum.

Over the decade history moved from 'rubies in porridge' to a prospering subject (OFSTED 1999). OFSTED inspectors noted a steady improvement in standards and in pupils' progress in history across both key stages. A large-scale, national research study showed that parents, as well as pupils and teachers, were enthusiastic about, for example, the way Roman and Greek history had developed Key Stage 2 children's understanding of concepts of change, and also their political and economic literacy, and literacy skills (Bage *et al.* 1999).

Yet there was already a dilemma arising. The second edition was published in response to the Revised National Curriculum (DfEE 1995b) which reduced the prescribed content and cumbersome assessment structure of the history curriculum. Although claims were made about increased opportunities for teachers' professional judgements in developing coherent balanced curricula reflecting the needs of individual schools, pupils and locations the subtext was the need to increase curriculum time spent on 'basic skills'. The National Strategies for Literacy (DfEE 1998a), Numeracy (DfEE 1999a) and an increased emphasis on Information and Communications Technology were already on the agenda, accompanied by target setting, testing and league tables which could not be ignored. In September 1998 legal requirements to teach all of the full Key Stage 1 and 2 programmes of study for history were 'relaxed' and guidance given for 'prioritising, combining and reducing the history curriculum' (QCA 1998a: 10–11), as teachers struggled to familiarise themselves with the literacy and numeracy frameworks.

This volte-face was echoed in the National Curriculum for Initial Teacher Training (DfEE 1998b). Increased emphasis on the core curriculum and on Information and Communications Technology reduced both the number of places allocated for training specialist students in the foundation subjects and also the time spent on these subjects by non-specialists.

It will be disastrous if, after all that has been achieved in developing life-enhancing history teaching by so many, and with such commitment during the 1990s history again becomes marginalised and superficial. There may not be the will, understanding or expertise to begin again when all the literacy targets have been reached (or not) and the curriculum is next revised.

This is amazing when we consider that the English National Curriculum for History is highly regarded in other countries. It has been influential in the development of history curricula in Europe, particularly in the countries of the former Communist bloc in Eastern Europe. At conferences in Strasbourg (Council of Europe 1995), Paris (Institut National de Recherche Pedagogique 1996), Frankfurt (European Conference of Educational Research 1997) and Brunswick (Georg Eckert Institut 1998),

When the English history curriculum was quoted everyone sits up. Ask questions? Discuss interpretations? Different media? Range of sources? How old are these children? Secondary pupils cannot do this, they say. They ask how it can be done. Can the pages be photocopied?

(*Times Educational Supplement*, 26 June 1998: 15).

So, in the third edition of *The Teaching of History in Primary Schools* there is an emphasis on investigating how history can also be linked to the requirements of the National Literacy, Numeracy and ICT requirements. For as these strategies become more familiar the creative opportunities for applying them to both the content and methods of enquiry across the curriculum become clear. If we can do this both basic skills and the foundation subjects are enhanced and the curriculum will be genuinely more coherent and enriched, for:

History...is a lively, challenging, indeed thrilling subject which deserves – and I would say has to be at the centre of any well balanced curriculum...the primary purpose of education is to produce well-rounded and sensitive human beings. If that is indeed our belief history must be central to the education of our children.

(Davies 1998: 5).

This third edition aims to support this process. The structure of the book is the same as in previous editions although each chapter has modifications. Chapter 1 discusses the nature of historical thinking which underpins history in the National Curriculum and includes an overview of resources produced since 1995 which support the implementation of the revised history curriculum. Chapter 2 gives an updated review of research investigating the kinds of thinking in history which young children may be capable of, and in this edition also shows how student teachers have used the research as a catalyst for identifying and investigated current questions related to their own practice. Chapter 3 describes the structure of the revised history order and considers the whole-school decisions involved in devising a scheme of work for its implementation. Case studies in Chapter 4 show how existing medium-term plans can be modified to bring them into line with the revisions, drawing on both evaluations of the existing curriculum and recent publications. The case studies in Chapter 5 are entirely new. They provide numerous examples of tutors on Initial Teacher Training courses working with students, teachers and children in schools to explore ways in which history can be linked to the national literacy and numeracy frameworks, and the ways in which the quality of history teaching can be enhanced through judicious use of Information and Communications Technology. Chapter 6 describes action research undertaken as a class teacher, based on studies described at the beginning of the book, and through this examines and encourages on-going dynamic links between theory and practice.

Chapter 1

Historical Thinking

Before history became a required part of the primary curriculum, history books for children did not take into account that, from the very beginning children are able, in a simple but genuinely historical way, to grapple with the problems that lie at the heart of the discipline and that they should so do in increasingly complex ways (Bruner 1963; Lawton 1975; Pring 1976). Often books made generalised and stereotypical statements and gave no indication of the sources on which these were based or of the areas of uncertainty in interpreting sources which influence any description, account or explanation of the past. Children were usually given a single perspective of the past and not helped to see why different people, at different times, create different interpretations which may be more or less valid. The concepts of time and change, motive, cause and consequence, similarity and difference were rarely developed.

> After they had been there for four hundred years, the Romans went away. Their homes in Italy were being attacked by fierce tribes and every soldier was needed. The Britons were sad when they went, for they had no soldiers of their own to protect them from the sea-raiders who were growing bolder in their attacks upon the coast.
>
> (Unstead 1964: 42)

Illustrations of artefacts were often presented as curious remnants rather than as rich sources from which a range of possible deductions may be made about the people who used them, and how their lives may have been influenced by them. 'Main events' and 'famous people' were listed at the back of a book simply because they happened, without apparent significance, and without conveying the idea that historians weave them together into accounts of the past, that they select and interpret them, and that this is why accounts may differ. (For current research on causation, and children's understanding of the reasons why the Romans conquered Britain see Lee (1998) and Lee *et al.* (1996a–d) referred to in Chapter 2.)

Children's active learning was often assumed to occur through 'Things to Do' at the end of a chapter, but this rarely involved a reconstruction based on real historical evidence, a real building or an archaeological site, and the inevitable questions this would raise. It is more likely to suggest that you 'Make a model Viking ship from stiff card or paper as shown below . . .' (Mitchell and Middleton 1967: 88). Alternatively, children were asked to 'Pretend you are a merchant living in Saxon times and tell of your adventure', which presupposes an understanding of attitudes, values and a social structure quite different from our own, or else invites anachronism and identification and so inhibits the development of true historical understanding. (Dickinson and Lee (1994) are also investigating young children's understanding of motive in the context of Anglo-Saxon oath-taking. This research is referred to in Chapter 2.)

Secondary sources for children were often written in unnecessarily obscure language.

> Drake is the most famous mariner in English history. He is renowned for his adventurous exploits as well as his enterprising skill in establishing the English navy as the country's main national weapon.
>
> (*Famous Sailors* 1970)

Yet history is not only concerned with great events or famous men. It encompasses all aspects of the lives of the men, women and children in a society. Historians attempt to find out about them through asking particular kinds of questions of whatever traces of the past remain.

The content of history

As David Thomson (1969) explained, history has developed over the last 200 years from chronicles of unrelated events into a discipline which aims to interpret different kinds of evidence in order to understand societies in the past. Its content is diverse: social, economic, constitutional, aesthetic. It may be concerned with individuals, institutions or groups. Philip Phenix (1964) saw history, with religion and philosophy, as forming a 'Realm of Meaning' which unites all other kinds of thinking. The National Curriculum takes account of this breadth of content.

It is the questions historians ask, however, and the ways in which they answer them, that distinguish history as a discipline. History is concerned with the causes and effects of change over time; with the ways in which, and the reasons why, societies in the past were different from ours, and what caused them to change. Historians investigate the past by interpreting traces of the past, the evidence. They interpret evidence through a process of deductive reasoning, but evidence is often incomplete, and for this and other reasons, more than one interpretation may be defensible. Producing a range of valid interpretations involves thinking which we may call 'historical imagination'. A wide and perceptive range of valid interpretations may eventually lead to an understanding of why people in the past may have thought, felt and behaved differently from us. Historical enquiry also depends on concepts which are, in varying degrees, peculiar to history. In this chapter, each of these aspects of historical thinking will be considered in turn. It is important to remember that they interact with each other in the process of finding out about the past.

The processes of historical enquiry

Making inferences about the past from evidence

There are many kinds of historical evidence: oral history, artefacts, pictures and photographs, maps, statistics, writing. Written evidence is wide-ranging: documents, laws, tombstone inscriptions, diaries, newspaper accounts, contemporary literature. Making historical inferences involves forming arguments about the significance of a piece of evidence: what does it tell us about the society that produced it? How was it made? Why? What was it used for? By whom? Where was it found? Are there others? . . . and so on.

Superior examples of Roman shoes found at Vindolanda, the equivalent of shoes made by Gucci or Lobbe today, tell us something about the social and economic structure of the fort. A letter from a first generation 'Dutch' Roman at the fort, written in Latin, asking for underpants and socks from Rome, may tell us about the economic and transport systems of the empire, and the attitudes of Dutch tribes to the cold, clothes and culture.

Since there is a limit to what can be known for certain, a historian must also make inferences which are probabilistic – reasonable guesses about the evidence. The four post-holes in the centre of an Iron Age house plan may be to support the roof (Bersu 1940), they may surround an open courtyard where animals could be kept (Clarke 1960), or they may be a free-standing tower for repairing the roof (Harding 1974).

If the evidence is incomplete, the historian must also be able to tolerate that which can never be known; for example, we do not know how much of a new style of agriculture the Romans introduced to Britain, or how it was related to the old, and so how British communities related to Roman villas, since no examples of Roman field patterns have been identified (Richmond 1955).

This process of enquiry in interpreting historical evidence was clarified by Collingwood in his autobiography (1939). He proceeded from specific questions about the significance and purpose of objects (whether they were buttons, dwellings or settlements), to their meaning for the people who made them. For instance, he knew that a Roman wall from the Tyne to Solway existed. He *guessed* its purpose was to form a sentry wall with parapets as a protection against snipers. He *wanted to know* if there were towers as a defence against trying to land at Bowness or St Bees, in order to support his guess. A search revealed that towers had been found, but their existence forgotten (because their purpose was not questioned).

Interpreting historical evidence involves not only internal argument, but also debate with others, testing inferences against evidence from other sources and considering other points of view. It means then supporting opinions with arguments, accepting that there is not always a 'right' answer, that there may be equally valid but different interpretations, and that some questions cannot be answered. This kind of thinking is as important to the social, emotional and intellectual growth of young children, as it is necessary in adult society.

Developing historical understanding

Interpreting historical evidence may involve suggesting how something was made, or used, or what it may have meant to people at the time. It may involve explaining a sequence of events or the behaviour of an individual or a group. Evidence is always incomplete. It is a reflection of the feelings and thoughts of the people who created it. Historical evidence is, therefore, often open to a variety of equally valid interpretations. In order to interpret evidence, it is necessary to understand that people in the past may have thought, felt and behaved differently from us, because they lived in societies with different knowledge-bases, belief-systems, views of the world, and different social, political and economic constraints. The disposition to make a variety of suggestions about incomplete evidence, which take into account that people in the past may have thought and felt differently from us, is therefore an integral part of making historical inferences. It has been called 'historical imagination' or 'historical empathy'. However, these terms have led to a great deal of confusion because they have often been regarded as the product of free-floating imagination discrete from interpreting evidence. They have also been confused with projecting oneself into the past, or with identifying or sympathising with people in the past. The historian cannot share the thoughts and feelings of people in the past but can attempt to understand and explain what these may have been. There has been confusion too, because the terms 'historical imagination' or 'empathy' involve a number of subordinate concepts: understanding different points of view in a conflict, the motives of an individual or a group, the values, attitudes and beliefs of another society.

Historians have an implicit understanding of historical imagination, which is usually not adequately articulated. Kitson Clarke (1967) pointed out that 'men's actions can be the subject of detailed research, but what went on in their minds can only be known by inference'. Elton (1970) saw historical imagination as 'a tool for filling in the gaps when facts are not available'. Ryle (1979) saw it as a means of cashing in on the facts and using them: ammunition shortage and heavy rain before a battle cause the historian to wonder about the hungry rifleman and delayed mule trains. Thomas (1983) said that what interests him about the past is what ordinary people thought, felt and believed. Collingwood (1939: 7) attempted to clarify the relationship between interpreting evidence and interpreting the thoughts and feelings of the people who made it. He says, for example, that we know that Julius Caesar invaded Britain in successive years; we can suppose that his *thoughts* may have been about trade, or grain supply, or a range of other possibilities, and that his underlying *feelings* may have included ambition or career advancement. (Mink (1968) rigorously analysed Collingwood's thinking on this subject in his article 'Collingwood's Dialectic of History'.)

Historians, then, do not question that making deductions about historical evidence involves probabilistic interpretations, and conjectures about thoughts, feelings and beliefs. Their job is not to reproduce the lost world of the past, but to ask questions and to try to answer them.

Nevertheless, it is important to recognise that suppositions about the feelings and thoughts of people who made and used historical evidence have to conform to criteria of validity. There must be no contradictory evidence. It must be assumed that people in the past acted rationally. Inferences must be supported by argument and conform to what else is known of the period. Historians must also attempt to understand what the evidence may have meant to people at the time. What, for example, was the status of a torc, dating from 1000 BC, discovered in a Wiltshire field? 'This may have been a votive offering to a God, or buried as part of a funeral ceremony, or it might have been stored' (Merriman, 1990).

Children can take part in the process of making suggestions about how things were made and used and how the people who used them may have thought and felt. They can be helped to imagine, for example, how it may have felt to do the washing using a copper, a dolly, a scrubber and a flat iron, to go to bed by candlelight, or to wear the clothes of children depicted in an old portrait. They can use parish registers, census records, street directories, old maps and information about daily life from secondary sources to reconstruct the life of a particular family living in a particular house at a given time in the past. They can suggest what life may have been like in seventeenth-century London after reading extracts from Pepys' diary, or how a Roman villa they have visited may have looked when it was first built. But the imaginative conjecture must be rooted in the evidence.

Children must be encouraged to 'go beyond the evidence' because this is central to developing historical understanding. Therefore they must gradually learn through discussion with each other and with their teacher how to make interpretations which are historically valid.

Using historical concepts

Historical evidence can only be interpreted through language. In order to ask questions of evidence, we need to use concepts which are in varying degrees peculiar to history. As Blyth (1990) pointed out, however, lists of historical concepts are drawn up almost arbitrarily. Some concepts are concerned with space and time, some are methodological: similarity and difference, cause and effect, continuity and change. Other concepts are organising ideas which run through human society: communication, power, beliefs, conflict. Concepts are created by historians to encapsulate historical periods: Renaissance, Reformation, Victorian. There are 'closed' concepts which refer to a particular time (villa, elderman, Roundhead, Cavalier), and concepts which are not exclusively historical (trade, law, agriculture).

Children need to be given the opportunity explicitly to discuss historical concepts, and to use them in a variety of contexts in interactive situations because these concepts form the framework which makes historical enquiry possible.

Why is it necessary for children in the primary school to learn the processes of historical thinking?

It is impossible to learn history without learning the processes by which historians find out about the past. There is no one view of the past, and historians' accounts of the past differ. To understand history, it is necessary to understand why these differences occur. It is necessary to understand that evidence from which accounts are constructed is incomplete and so more than one interpretation is usually possible. Therefore, historians write accounts of the past which involve both selecting and interpreting evidence, in order to explain what happened and why. The areas they choose to investigate, the evidence they select, their interpretations of the feelings and thoughts which lie behind actions, and the patterns of events they construct often differ. They may vary as a result of the historian's interests, the concerns and philosophies of the times in which s/he lives, or the discovery of new evidence. A Marxist historian like

Christopher Hill, for example, will write a different account of the English Civil War from that of C. V. Wedgewood. Recent historians (Fryer 1984, 1989; Vishram 1988; Rodney 1972) have challenged an Anglocentric view of history. Others have taken a woman's perspective (Boulding 1981; Beddoe 1983; Rowbotham 1973).

History is dynamic. In learning about the past through secondary sources, children will discover that accounts differ, and in asking their own questions about primary sources, they will begin to discover why. It is important to social and intellectual development, not solely to historical understanding, to realise that arguments must be supported and that there is often no one 'right' answer.

The National Curriculum created a focus and structure for the development of a rich variety of materials to support genuine historical enquiry at Key Stages 1 and 2. These all remain valid, although with experience the ways in which they are used has been modified. A major new series published since 1995 is the Cambridge Primary History (McAleavy 1997) in which activities are clearly rooted in research into the development of children's understanding in history, and allow for differentiation and progression. Other publishers have produced new additions to history topics. *Ancient African Town – Benin* (MacDonald and Wood 1999) is a good example. This is part of the expanding Metropolis series from Franklin Watts. History in Evidence has continued to produced replica sources of all kinds. New books on the teaching of history have been published. Often authors have worked in partnership with teachers to find ways of applying theory and research to develop practice in teaching the National Curriculum: Wood and Holden 1995; Fines and Nichol 1997; Nichol and Dean 1997; Davidson 1997. Claire (1996) has shown how an inclusive history curriculum can be developed for the primary school; this is one of the stated key objectives of the 2000 curriculum. Others have debated lively issues concerning the content and implementation of the National History Curriculum in 2000 and beyond (Jenkins 1995; Arthur and Phillips 2000; Husbands 1996; Phillips 1998).

The Historical Association magazines, *Primary History* and *Teaching History* continue to flourish. The major new resource for teaching the 2000 curriculum however, is multimedia. The BBC Video Plus series has been produced in boxed sets with supporting materials: Within Living Memory (0 563 46230), Tudor Life (0 563 462175), Time-Lines: Teaching Chronology (0 563 462132). CD Roms such as Houses and Householders (Anglia Multimedia) are accompanied by glossy books. The Interfact Series (Two-Can Publishing) covers disks on The Romans, Aztecs, Egyptians and Vikings, which involve geography and science as well as history. The opportunities offered by the proliferation of history web sites are discussed in Chapter 5.

Official guidance since 1995 has been concerned with showing teachers how to link history to other subjects (SCAA 1997) and to teach and assess it in focused ways (QCA 1998b; 2000), in order to manage curriculum time most effectively since the introduction of the literacy and numeracy hours. The National Curriculum (2000) identifies explicit links between history, English, mathematics and ICT.

Recent publications explore the links between history and other subjects, while retaining the concepts, questions and ways of answering them which lie at the heart of history. Roberts (1998) has produced materials which show how the literacy hour can be taught using paintings as an historical source and Arnold and Slater (1999), give very clear plans for teaching a sequence of literacy hours using Victorian written sources. A variety of written sources which could be used in this way to teach other history study units has been selected by Blyth and Hughes (1997). In *Narrative Matters* (1999) Bage exemplifies theory through practical examples which show how stories set in the past can be a powerful means of teaching history. In *History and English in the Primary School* (Hoodless 1998) a combination of academics and teachers apply sound research evidence through a series of case studies to show, in practical, interesting and innovative ways, how learning history can also promote literacy objectives. The Literacy Through History project at Exeter University explores links between history topics and the literacy hour through on-going action research (Nichol 1998).

Books will inevitably follow which explore links between history and other curriculum areas. Case studies linking history, music and ICT and history and mathematics are given in Chapter 5. But 'if a strong case can be made that history is not only important for cultivating literacy but is actually essential for the promotion of creative, well argued and substantiated writing, communication and language, then the literacy strategy has exciting potential for the teaching of history in primary schools' (Phillips 1999).

Chapter 2
Historical Thinking and Cognitive Development

Apparently some readers of previous editions have found this chapter daunting. This may be so, but it is an attempt to summarise theories of cognitive development and to link these to research into the development of children's thinking in history. Theories evolve through research, through raising questions and finding ways of answering them. The best questions are asked and the most useful information collected by those with a professional understanding of the issues, in everyday contexts. Reflecting on, analysing and evaluating practice lies at the heart of personal and professional growth and judgement. This in turn informs, refines and modifies existing theory. As the research described in this chapter makes clear, there is much more to be learned about what constitutes good teaching strategies (appropriate materials, questions, tasks) and about progression in and assessment of children's learning in history.

So in this edition we examine theories of cognitive development relevant to each aspect of historical thinking: making inferences, historical imagination and concept development. Research which relates each area to children's thinking in history is discussed, then in addition some examples are given of how student teachers during their final block placement on a BA (QTS) course used these research studies as a catalyst for investigations into their own teaching. These investigations relate previous research to real current dilemmas. They demonstrate reflection on practice and the dynamic links between theory and practice. Those quoted are only a stimulus for the infinite opportunities students and teachers can create for their own investigations.

Theories of cognitive development relevant to making historical inferences

Piaget posited a sequence in the development of children's thinking encompassing three qualitative stages. This is consistent with the view that children become increasingly able to make inferences about the past from historical sources. Young children, he found, were not able to hold more than one perspective at a time. At the next stage children's thinking was bound by observable reality. At the third stage they were able to hold in mind a range of hypothetical possibilities.

Piaget's research on probability and chance (Piaget and Inhelder 1951) is based on the manipulation of physical objects, predicting the colour of marbles to be drawn from a bag, or rolled down a tray. However, it is interesting that he found that while young children make no differentiation between chance and non-chance, at a concrete level children show an increasing awareness of what they can know and what they can guess, so that at a formal level, they are able to establish a firm bridge between the certain and the probable.

Piaget's work on language (1926) and on logic (1928) is the most helpful to apply to inferential reasoning in history. Here he sets out a sequence in the development of argument. In *The Language and Thought of the Child* (1926) he says that at the egocentric level, the child is not concerned with interesting or convincing others, and leaps from a premise to an unreasonable conclusion in one bound. Next s/he attempts to communicate intellectual processes which are factual and descriptive, and show incipient logic, but this is not clearly expressed. This leads to a valid statement of fact or description. From this follows 'primitive argument' in which the statement or opinion is followed by a deduction going beyond the information given, but the explanation for the deduction is only implicit. At the next stage, the child attempts to justify and demonstrate his/her assertion by using a conjunction (since, because, therefore), but does not succeed in expressing a truly logical relationship. Piaget says, in *Judgement and Reasoning in the Child*:

> The young child (7–8) rarely spontaneously uses 'because' or 'although' and, if forced to finish sentences using them, uses them as a substitute for 'and then'.
> (Piaget 1928)

The child eventually arrives at 'genuine argument', through frequent attempts to justify his/her own opinions and avoid contradiction, and as the result of internal debate, s/he is able to use 'because' and 'therefore' correctly to relate an argument to its premise. Finally, at a formal level, s/he can use not only conjunctions, but also disjunctions, can make implications and consider incompatible propositions.

This pattern in the development of argument has been examined, assessed and modified by subsequent research. Peel (1960) identified a 'describer' stage of unjustified and unqualified statements, a transitional stage of justified hypothesis and a recognition of logical possibilities, and an 'explainer' stage of weighed arguments using abstract propositions.

Nevertheless, young children's ability to make inferences may be greater than Piaget suggested. It often seems to be limited by lack of knowledge or experience, or failure to understand the kind of thinking that is expected. In history it would vary, depending on the nature of the evidence. Piaget and Inhelder themselves (Peel 1960) found levels of thinking varied according to the nature of the questions asked.

A child's interest and involvement are also important as Beard (1960) showed. Isaacs (1948) found very young children capable of logical argument if they understood how to tackle the problem and were interested in it. Wheeler (Peel 1960) found that logical thinking can exist from an early age, and that it becomes more complex through increased experience and memory. Piaget's own case studies offer some evidence that comments, suggestions and criticisms make pupils aware of the elements in problem-solving, and can accelerate their progress. Donaldson (1978) examined the dichotomy she recognised between children's capacity for reasoning in informal, everyday situations and Piaget's conclusion that children under seven have little reasoning ability. She found that young children are capable of deductive reasoning, that their problem-solving depends on the extent to which they can concentrate on language, and that language development is related to other non-verbal clues which are also brought to bear in problem-solving. She found that children may encounter difficulties because they do not always select relevant items in problem-solving, are easily distracted, and rarely discuss the meaning of words. She concluded that a child's understanding depends on whether the reasoning stems from the child's immediate concerns or is externally imposed, and also on the child's expectation of what the questioner wants to know. She said, therefore, that young children must be helped to develop their ability to reason and to make inferences as early as possible by recognising the abstraction of language, and by receiving the right kind of help in problem-solving. They must also become aware of the nature of different disciplines.

Psychologists' work on reasoning, then, suggests that young children may be helped to develop arguments about historical evidence if we teach them how. It suggests that we need to provide interesting, memorable learning experiences, ask simple, open-ended questions, and teach appropriate vocabulary. Recent research (e.g. Kerry 1998) draws on constructivist learning theory to analyse types and categories of teachers' and pupils' questions and their impact on pupil learning. It will be very interesting to apply this to questioning on history.

Research relating psychologists' work on making inferences to children's thinking in history

There have been studies relating Piaget's developmental levels to children's historical thinking. However, they have found that the three levels can be revealed among a group of children of almost any age, because the nature of the evidence and the complexity of the questions influences children's level of response. Since the studies have usually involved older children, they are of limited value to primary school teachers. Nevertheless, they have been encouraging in recognising approaches to teaching history which have been successful, in establishing that young children enjoy making inferences about historical evidence, and in focusing attention on the quality of children's thinking rather than simply on fact acquisition.

In the 1960s, children's responses to historical evidence were classified in terms of Piagetian levels by Lodwick (1958 in Peel 1960: 121), Thompson (1972), Peel (1960), Booth (1969), Hallam (1975) and Rees (1976). Lodwick's study is perhaps the most useful to those interested in young children because it involved visual evidence and did not depend on understanding individuals' motives, or on causation. He showed children between 7 and 14 a picture of Stonehenge and asked them three questions, for example: 'Do you think Stonehenge might have been a temple or a fort?' Their answers showed a gradual development from unreason to logic, then the use of supporting evidence, and probabilistic thinking. Eventually, they were able both to support a hypothesis that it was a temple, and also to argue as to why it was not a fort. The answers suggest that the development in reasoning is due, to some extent, to an increase in knowledge. More information might therefore have enabled the children to argue logically at an earlier age.

Thompson (1972) gave a mixed ability class of 12-year-old boys background information about William the Conqueror, then gave them extracts from the *Domesday Book* and from the *Anglo-Saxon Chronicle*, and asked them why William had the survey carried out. This material is far more complex than that of Lodwick, because it involves written evidence, comparing two sources, and understanding both bias and motive. It also involves understanding a society with different rules. At a preoperational level replies showed misunderstanding of the information. At a concrete level children repeated information given in the chronicle. Formal responses showed awareness of uncertainty and probability, an understanding of the King's insecure position, and of his need not to be cheated of taxes. Piaget's work on rules and motives (1932) showed that by 12 years old, children can understand that rules can be changed, they take account of motive, and see that justice is relative. Piaget says this is achieved through comparing and discussing perspectives. However, Thompson (1972) seems to have found some children operating at a fairly low level because of the abstraction and complexity of the material, and also perhaps because he required a written response.

It is not surprising that Peel (1960) traced the same three Piagetian levels of response among a group of junior school children when he asked a far more simple question about a story. He told them the story of King Alfred and the cakes, and asked them, 'Could Alfred cook?' Indeed, this is hardly an historical question and requires no understanding of laws, motive, bias or of another society. Peel found that at seven, children's answers were often illogical ('Yes, he was King', or, 'No, he could fight'). At a concrete level, they would restate evidence in the story, but at a transitional level they may state what might be expected ('I shouldn't think so – at least not as well. He didn't pay attention to the cakes. If he had been a good cook he might have known when they'd be done'). At a formal level, they may state a possibility not given in the text ('I don't know, because if anyone could cook and had something else on his mind, he might still forget the cakes'). Peel's responses might have been analysed in a more refined way, appropriate to the age-range if his categories had reflected Piaget's sequence in *The Language and Thought of the Child* (1926): egocentric, incipient logic, statements of fact, implicit deduction, incomplete causal relationship, genuine argument.

Booth (1969) constructed tests for 13- to 14-year-olds, designed to explore the nature of their knowledge of history. They were asked questions about time and change, and about the attitudes, ideas and beliefs represented by three religious buildings of different periods. They were also asked to compare and contrast people, events and photographs of houses from different periods. Booth, too, found that answers fell into three categories: those that had little or no comprehension of the material or the questions, those that referred to the information given but made little attempt to refer to historical material outside the question; and those that showed selection and critical thinking and related their work to other relevant knowledge. Such questions and material could easily be adapted for primary school children, and if related to a unit of study, would most likely receive responses at the two higher levels, although their answers may be different from those of 13-year-olds.

It seems that researchers tried to fit their children's responses into Piaget's three bands, irrespective of age group or material, rather than ask simple, open-ended questions and see what patterns emerged.

It is interesting that Booth found more divergent thinking and flexibility when children were asked questions orally and pupils' questionnaires showed that they enjoyed class discussion, local history studies, and examining pictures, documents and maps, and disliked facts, generalisations and 'essay' writing.

In the 1970s, experiments and strategies were designed to see if children's thinking in history could be accelerated within the Piagetian model by teaching methods. Hallam (1975) worked with 9- and 13-year-olds and Rees (1976) with 12-year-olds.

Hallam taught 'experimental' classes through active problem-solving in role-play ('Imagine you are Henry VIII and say why you have decided to abolish the monasteries'), through asking questions about Cromwell's diary and discussing passages from historical texts. He found that the classes taught through active problem-solving performed at a higher level than the traditionally taught control group.

Rees (1976) also found that children's thinking skills in history could be developed if they were taught to explain rather than describe, and to be aware of uncertainty and motive, by switching perspective. His classes of 12-year-olds compared favourably at the end of the term with a control group who were taught in a didactic way. Rees found three levels of response to his fairly complex material. Answers requiring inference were considered to be preoperational if no explanation was given, at a concrete level if only one explanatory reference was given, and at a formal level if all explanatory references were given. Responses to questions requiring pupils to take account of two points of view fell into three categories: those which showed no logic, those which showed increasing quantities of substantiating evidence but only in support of one viewpoint, and those that appreciated two viewpoints.

Dickinson and Lee (1978: 82) concentrated on defining historical thinking, rather than Piagetian levels, as the starting point. They made clear for the first time the important distinction between understanding behaviour from a contemporary viewpoint and from the standpoint available to the person at the time. They gave adolescents some of the information available to Jellico before the Battle of Jutland and asked them why he turned back. They traced a sequence in the development of the pupils' understanding that there is a difference between Jellico's point of view and that of the historian.

Shemilt (1980) worked with 13- to 16-year-olds. He found that children taught through active problem-solving are less inclined to regard 'facts' as certain. He suggested the following pattern of development: evidence as 'information', as giving answers to be unearthed, as presenting problems to work out, and finally as recognition that the context of evidence is necessary to establish historicity.

Although this research is interesting because it shows that it is possible to develop genuine historical thinking, it gives the impression that this is only possible with older children. However, with simpler material and questions, these approaches could be adapted for younger children. It seems important therefore to define, through teachers' experience, based on planning for precise learning outcomes, the historical questions and kinds of evidence appropriate at different ages, and to look, in a much more refined way at children's responses to them.

Shawyer, Booth and Brown (1988) noted that although there had been greater use of sources in the last ten years, there had been little research into children's levels of understanding of the evidence. Three small-scale studies investigated young children's ability to make inferences about evidence; they did not attempt to explore the range of children's thinking in detail, but they did suggest that it is possible to teach strategies which stimulate the building blocks of advanced historical thinking in young children.

Wright (1984) found that classes of seven-year-old children could draw their own conclusions about pottery 'finds' from the past; Davis (1986) asked junior school children to identify 'mystery objects' and found they could make historical statements which were tentative and provisional. Hodgkinson (1986) showed genuine historical objects (e.g. newspapers, candle-holders) and 'fake' historical objects (e.g, mock ship's log), to children of nine and ten years old. He, too, found they used probability words and used 'because' to develop an argument. Marbeau (1988) concluded that in primary school history, we must provide a means for open and animated thought so that the child has intellectual autonomy, can take risks, exchange ideas and organise thoughts relative to the thoughts of others. In this way, a plan or a photograph can come to life

Student teachers investigate children's inferences about sources

Paula Andrews, a student teacher, wanted to find out how to bring a collection of historical artefacts to life in this way for her Key Stage 1 class. The National Curriculum says that they should learn to 'ask and answer questions about the past' but what sorts of questions should they be encouraged to ask and what is the teacher's role? Is there a progression in the type of questions for Year 1 to Year 2? Which artefacts stimulate the most questions, and why? She found that the youngest children made observations and needed help to turn these into questions; as they got older they were able to formulate their own questions and increasingly they asked open questions which led to discussions: how things were made, how they were used, why? She found the artefacts which provoked most interest and discussion in her Year 1/2 class were things which worked and could be explored through manipulation.

When Beverley Wright, another student, asked her Year 3/4 class to make inferences about the people depicted in a selection of Tudor portraits she did this through a literacy hour on adjectives but also used this opportunity to contest gender stereotypes. She, like Claire (1996), found that children attributed strengths and weaknesses to male and female portraits respectively and used the plenary session to discuss this with them and challenge their assumptions.

Theories of cognitive development relevant to historical imagination

There are three aspects of developmental psychology which seem relevant to the development of historical imagination: work on 'creative thinking', work on changing perspective, and theories of psychodynamics.

The first area, 'creative thinking', has implications for how children may best be encouraged to make a range of valid suppositions about evidence (how it was made and used, and what it meant to people at the time).

Since the 1960s, psychologists who were concerned that traditional intelligence tests were too narrow a measure of intellectual ability, have devised creativity tests. Creativity however was also difficult to define. Rogers (1959) saw it as 'growing out of the interaction of the individual and his material'. Guilford (1959) listed traits related to creativity: the ability to see a problem, fertility of ideas, word-fluency, expressional fluency, and fluency of ideas (the ability to produce ideas to fulfil certain requirements such as uses for a brick, in limited time), flexible thinkers who could produce a variety of ideas, or solve unusual problems (which of the following objects could be adapted to make a needle – a radish, fish, shoe, carnation?), and tolerance of ambiguity, a willingness to accept some uncertainty in conclusions.

Guilford devised tests to measure such abilities. Other tests of creativity followed. Torrance (1965) used an 'Ask and Guess' test requiring hypotheses about causes and results related to a picture, and a 'just suppose' test in which an improbable situation in a drawing requires imaginative solutions. Wallach and Kagan (1965) said that creativity can be tested by the number of associates, and the number of unique associates generated in response to given tests, both verbal and visual. Their tests included interpretation of visual patterns and suggesting uses for objects such as a cork or a shoe. Researchers concluded that creativity is a dimension which involves a child's ability to generate unique and plentiful associates in a task-appropriate manner, and in a relatively playful context. Such research has implications for classroom practice. It is generally accepted that the ability to think creatively rather than conform without question is important for individual and social well-being. Teachers can develop divergent thinking both through creative problem-solving courses (Parnes 1959), and by creating an environment in which children become confident in their ability to think adventurously (Haddon and Lytton 1968). On the other hand, Torrance (1962), Wallach and Kagan (1965), and Getzels and Jackson (1962) showed that highly creative children are often not encouraged or recognised by their teachers, who prefer conformity.

The second area of psychologists' work which may shed light on children's ability to understand how people in the past may have felt, thought and behaved is concerned directly with empathy. However, psychologists' definitions of empathy are of limited use when applied to history because they are partial, misleading or irrelevant. Piaget saw it as a cognitive process, thinking rather than feeling from someone else's point of view. His 'Three Mountains' experiment (1956) suggested that young children find this difficult, but others have said that it depends on their involvement, and on their understanding of the situation. J. H. Flavell (1985) suggested that children are capable of making inferences which enable them to see someone else's point of view, but do not see the need to do so. This is endorsed by Martin Hughes' 'Policeman Replication' of the Three Mountains experiment (Donaldson 1978) and by the 'Sesame Street test' of H. Borke (1978).

Recent research differentiates between visual perspective-taking, conversational role-taking and pictorial representation, and in each instance, young children appear to be underestimated. Cox (1986) said that in their verbal interactions, young children do develop inferences concerning the points of view of others, but more research is needed into the intervening years between early childhood and maturity.

Piaget (1932) suggested the sequence in which children learn about rules: at first they do not understand that rules exist, then they change them according to their own needs. Next they come to accept one set of rules rigidly. Finally they are able to understand that rules change as society changes and are not absolute. In historical terms, they first become able to see life from another standpoint, but only with maturity can they understand that rules and behaviour change with society.

The third area of psychologists' work which has a bearing on how we should develop children's historical imagination is concerned with psychodynamics. Jones' (1968) approach was based on the work of Erikson (1965). He criticised Bruner's emphasis on deductive reasoning, divorced from emotional involvement. Jones thought that children must be encouraged to understand both themselves and the behaviour, feelings and ideas of different societies and that it is essential that cognitive development should be related to emotional and imaginative growth. 'It is necessary that children feel myth as well as understand it' (1968: 49). He asked children, for example, to list the kinds of conflicts to be expected in a Netsilik winter camp and how they are solved (through food-sharing, games, taboos and magic), then to categorise their own conflicts and ways of solving them.

Theories relating to historical empathy regard it as both a cognitive and an affective process, although the relationship between these processes and the pattern of their development is unclear. Watts (1972) stressed the constant interaction of deductive reasoning with imaginative thinking in history. The work of some psychologists has shown that the creativity needed to make valid suppositions, and the ability to suggest another person's point of view requires reasoning, but psychodynamic theories show that such reasoning involves an exploration of creative fantasy, an understanding of our own feelings and of how these are part of shared human experience.

Bruner, while still holding firmly to earlier views about the importance of structuring subjects, the spiral curriculum and self-generated discovery in learning a subject, has recently re-emphasised the importance of narrative and story-making in helping children, or indeed adults, to create a vision of the world, past and present, in which psychologically speaking they can envisage a place for themselves. One aspect of historical understanding, he says, comes through retelling a story of what something is about.

> Understanding, unlike explaining, is not pre-emptive. One way of construing the fall of Rome narratively does not preclude other ways.
>
> (Bruner 1996: 90)

Narratives, Bruner argues, can derive from competing perspectives and still be principled if they are well argued, documented and perspectively honest and it is, he says, a lame excuse to say that kids can't participate in this process (1996: 91).

Research investigating the development of historical imagination in children

There have been three studies which suggest that in history, children become increasingly able to make suppositions, to understand other points of view and values different from their own.

Blakeway (1983) constructed tasks which she felt made 'human sense' (Donaldson 1978), were age-appropriate (Borke 1978), and which made children aware of different perspectives and of the need to communicate them (Knight 1989c). In the first part of her study, she showed that her class of nine-year-olds could understand the pain and uncertainty of evacuees in the Second World War, and could also understand the thoughts and feelings which might have been experienced by an adult, a fighter pilot. However, the attempt to give the material 'human sense' in that it involved children not long ago, in the same school, meant that the children were more likely to sympathise and identify, than to display an understanding of different attitudes and values. In the second part of her study, she investigated the ability of two classes of eight- and nine-year-olds to make inferences. She asked them, 'What would you have felt if you were the fifteen-year-old King, Richard II, fighting the rebels in the Peasants' Revolt? Would you agree to their demands?' She found that the emotions ascribed to the King were limited to the children's own experience of life. This is not surprising since the difference between feeling fear, jealousy and anger depends on a person's perception of the situation. The older children offered more possible interpretations of the King's reasons and three-quarters of them were able to suggest why they might have gone to London, if they had been peasants. Blakeway's study (1983) shows that, by stopping to consider choice, children become aware of the possibilities that are available, they have control over their thinking, and become able to generate a variety of suppositions which lead towards understanding another point of view.

Knight (1989a; b) traced the emergence, in sequence, of four different aspects of children's understanding of people in the past. He tape-recorded 95 children between 6 and 14. He found that the first competency to emerge was the ability to retell a story from the point of view of someone involved in it. Six-year-olds found this difficult, but 67 per cent of the sample could do this by 9.3 years and 80 per cent by 10.3 years old. Next, children became able to explain an apparently strange attitude. They were told the story of General Wolfe, who died after finally capturing Quebec from the French. Then they were asked why he said 'Now I die happy'. Thirty-two per cent of six- and eight-year-olds offered nonsensical explanations, accepting that he was unaware of the dangers and also deterred by them. The older children (67 per cent by 9.4 years, 80 per cent by 12.8 years) accepted that people are driven by reasons and do what seems sensible to them and they also displayed an appreciation of a range of possibilities. The primary school children were not successful on the other two tasks, where they were asked to predict the ending of a story, and to interpret equivocal information about William I. Knight concluded, like Blakeway, that primary school children have sufficient understanding of people in the past to be worth encouraging, and that they are capable of making a range of valid suppositions. However, both these studies involve understanding accounts and motives of individuals in complex situations. It seems likely that attempts to understand the possible feelings and thoughts of people in the past begin to emerge much earlier.

Attempts to classify levels of historical empathy in adolescents have involved understanding of beliefs and complex social practices, and so have been less encouraging in their findings to primary practitioners. Ashby and Lee (1987) made video recordings of small-group discussions among 11- to 14-year-olds, in which no teacher was present, about Anglo-Saxon oath-taking and ordeals. At the first level, Anglo-Saxons were seen as simple; and their behaviour as absurd. At the next level, there are stereotyped role descriptions, with no attempt to distinguish between what people now know and think, and what they knew and thought in the past. At the level of every day empathy, there is a genuine attempt to reconstruct a situation and to project themselves into it and a recognition that beliefs, values and goals were different. At the fifth level, there is a clear understanding that people in the past had different points of view, institutions and social practices, and an attempt to understand what a person may have believed, in order to act in a particular way.

Research into young children's thinking in history suggests that, in a limited way, they can make suppositions about how people in the past may have felt and thought. However, this research has been concerned with motives and actions and has not investigated how children may make suppositions about evidence, artefacts, oral evidence, pictures or archaeological sites, in order to understand the thoughts and feelings of the people who made and used them.

Student teachers investigate links between inferences about sources and historical imagination

Following the introduction of the literacy hours in 1999 several students decided to investigate the interaction which had been noted by Jones (1968) and Watts (1972) between deductive reasoning and imaginative thinking in history, through historical fiction. Kathleen Watson worked with Year 5/6 children in six schools. They read either *Carrie's War* (Bawden 1973), a fictional story set in World War II, or a selection of non-fiction texts about the war. Kathleen constructed a questionnaire and interview schedule for 64 of the children and found that, although in the short term the children who read the non-fiction text remembered more factual information, over a longer period this was more true of the fiction readers. 'Was this because they were more imaginatively engaged with the thoughts and feelings of people in a previous time and this made the factual information more meaningful and memorable?' she wondered. We look forward to your next study Kathleen!

Alison Taylor read her Key Stage 1 children the Greek legend of the Minotaur. They discussed fact and fiction, then used reference books to find out how to make the 'flats' for a cardboard-box theatre and card-stick puppets in order to present their play, *The Minotaur*. In doing so they accurately represented the harbour, buildings, ships and dress of Ancient Crete. The play was written with due attention to spelling and punctuation, phonics and sound blends!

Dawn Ramsdale helped children to make suppositions about how people in the past may have thought and felt, and to consider points of view and attitudes different from their own through a variety of drama techniques: hot-seating, still images and role-play.

Paul Hutchinson investigated the role of historical imagination in developing historical understanding in relation to another topical issue, the appropriate use of video in teaching history. He found that his Year 4 class learned most from reconstructions: Tudor houses being built, life on Tudor ships, preparation for a Tudor feast. And they identified most with the children in their reconstructions, often relating them to their own experiences, and recreating them in their own role-play. Bage (1999) has suggested innumerable ways in which we can further explore the links between developing historical imagination and interpreting historical sources through story.

Psychologists' research into the development of concepts

The wide-ranging nature of historical concepts and also the need for children to learn to use the vocabulary of history, has already been discussed (see p. 6).

Psychologists have investigated both the sequence in which concept understanding develops and how concepts are learned, and this work has important implications for teachers.

Vygotsky (1962) showed that concepts are learned, not through ready-made definitions, but through trial and error, and experience. Concept development is a deductive process. The stages in which concepts are learned, not surprisingly, therefore correspond to those of Piaget. At the first stage, objects are linked by chance. At the second stage, they are linked by one characteristic, which can change as new information is introduced; children's and adults' words may seem to coincide but the child may be thinking of the concept in a different way; they may have a different understanding of what is meant by, for example, king, palace, peasant or law. At the final stage, a child is able to formulate a rule which establishes a relationship between other concepts and so creates an abstract idea; spears, daggers, guns, missiles are used for defence and attack; they are weapons. Klausmeier and Allen (1978), Klausmeier *et al.* (1979), Ausubel (1963; 1968) and Gagne (1977) endorsed this process and the levels of understanding, with 'concrete' and directly experienced concepts preceding abstract ones, although this is not always the case, or true for all concepts.

Vygotsky suggested that concept development can be promoted by careful use of language. It is particularly significant for teachers of history that he said that concepts which are specially taught because they belong to a particular discipline and are not acquired spontaneously are learned more consciously and completely. The significant use of a new concept promotes intellectual growth. Shif (1935) found that in social studies, when given sentence fragments ending in 'because', more children were able to complete the sentence using a concept consciously learned than using a spontaneous concept related to family situations. They understood 'exploitation' better than 'cousin'. He concluded that this was because the teacher had encouraged them to use 'because' consciously and explained new concepts, supplied information, questioned and corrected, and so these concepts had been learned in the process of instruction in collaboration with an adult.

Klausmeier *et al.* (1979) discussed how concrete, tangible concepts are learned through verbal labelling and through storing images; for example through discussing the characteristics of Tudor houses, the different parts of the timber frame, the wattle, brick, thatch, jetties, pargeting, and by storing images of a range of different examples, language both connects and differentiates the images. As children get older, language becomes more important than visual and tactile perceptions. Abstract concepts are formed by asking a series of questions: What is an axe, a scraper, a flake or an awl used for? Why? How? What is their common purpose? What is a bow, harpoon, spear used for? Why? How? What do they have in common? Then the former are 'tools' and the latter are 'weapons'. Concepts such as 'control' or 'power' involve understanding subordinate abstract concepts; understanding things which give people power (concepts such as tools and weapons), things that have power over people (fear of hunger, illness, natural phenomena), and also the things people might quarrel about.

Research has shown then that concepts are best learned if they are selected and specially taught through illustrations, using visual or tactile examples of concrete concepts, and discussion of abstract concepts. Psychologists have therefore also considered the kinds of material children should be given to discuss and how these discussions may be promoted.

Bruner (1966) postulated three modes of representation in understanding a body of knowledge: 'enactive', depending on physical experience or sensation (a visit to a site maybe or using a tool or other artefact), 'iconic', when the essence of the experience is represented in pictures in the mind's eye (paintings, maps, diagrams, models), and 'symbolic', when concepts are organised in symbols or in language. He saw these three kinds of understanding as complementary rather than rigidly successive. Bruner (1963) said that the questions children are asked about the material must be not too trivial, not too hard, and must lead somewhere, and that we need to know more about the ways in which this can be done. He said that this needs particularly sensitive judgement in history, which is characterised by uncertainty, ambiguity and probability. They must be asked about carefully selected evidence, so that general principles can be inferred from specific instances, connections can be made, and detail can be placed in a structured pattern which is not forgotten. A young child, he said, must be given minimal information, and emphasis on how s/he can go beyond it. Having selected the experience, material and questions carefully, the child must also be shown how to answer them. Learning a particular way of formulating and answering questions may be an essential step towards understanding conceptual ideas.

Little was done to put these principles into practice. Reports (DES 1978; 1982; 1989) showed that children were seldom taught to present a coherent argument, explore alternative possibilities, and draw conclusions. However, since the invention of the small, portable tape-recorder, there has been considerable research investigating discussion. There is evidence that a tape-recorder encourages 'on-task' behaviour and clear expression of ideas (Barnes and Todd 1977; Richmond 1982; Schools Council 1979).

Piaget argued (1932; 1950) that conflicting viewpoints encourage the ability to consider more than one perspective at a time, and Vygotsky (1962) saw the growth of understanding as a collective process. Rosen and Rosen (1973: 32) and Wade (1981) discuss the nature of group conversations with or without the teacher. Indeed, there is evidence that if children are taught the kinds of questions to ask and appropriate ways of answering them, their discussions without the teacher are in many ways more valuable. Biott (1984) found that such discussions were more dense, discursive and reflective. Prisk (1987) found that when the teacher was present in an informal group, children did not use their organisational skills since the teacher was responsible for 80 per cent of the structuring moves. She found that open, unled discussion encouraged children to produce tentative suggestions and to explore ideas, entertain alternative hypotheses, and evaluate each other's contribution. Nevertheless, adult–child interaction is important if it is not used to transmit didactic information, but in order to help children to understand a question and how to answer it.

Current research argues that cognition is intrinsically social. Hamlyn (1982) argued that discussion is necessary, though not sufficient for knowledge: 'To understand that something is true presupposes knowing what is meant by true'. This involves appreciation of standards of correction and so implies correction by others, and so the context of personal relations. Knowledge is also always a matter of degree in the sense that two people may know 'x' (in 1492 Columbus sailed the ocean blue), but one may know more of why this is significant than the other. They may both know that Charles I was beheaded in 1649 but one may understand more of the reasons why. Doise *et al.* (1975), Doise (1978) and Doise and Mugny (1979) saw cognitive growth as the result of conflict of viewpoint and of interaction at different cognitive levels. Ashby and Lee (1987) found that children reached higher levels of understanding when arguing out a problem among themselves than they could achieve on their own, both in class discussion and in small-group work, providing they had some strategy for tackling it.

Over the past 15 years there has been a great deal of generic research investigating the role of whole-class and group discussion in promoting learning (e.g. Bennett and Dunne 1992; Galton and Williamson 1992, National Oracy Project 1992). Research into effective questioning has explored ways in which children can learn to speculate, consider reasons, causes, motives, formulate ideas, use specialised vocabulary, contribute and listen to the views of others, analyse, synthesise and reach informed conclusions (Brown and Wragg 1993; Kerry 1998).

The National Curriculum 2000 stresses the importance of key skills of communication: contribution to small-group and whole-class discussion, reflection and critical evaluation, opportunities to consider different perspectives and to benefit from what others think and do across the curriculum and key stages.

Research applying theories of concept development to children's use of historical concepts

There have been studies investigating children's understanding of historical concepts: concepts of time, concepts often used in history but not related to a particular period, specifically historical vocabulary, and concepts related to the processes of historical thinking.

Concepts of time

First let us consider research dealing with children's concepts of time. The work of Piaget (1956) suggested that since the concept of time can only be understood in relation to concepts of speed, movement and space, and since understanding this relationship develops slowly, young children cannot understand that time can be measured in equal intervals. Piaget's work on time (1956) is not the most useful to apply to history. He investigated the development of concepts of time in relation to concepts of space, movement and velocity, through scientific experiments. Children were asked, for instance, to draw a succession of pictures showing water pouring from one container, through a spigot, into a container below. He found the first competency to emerge was the ability to match pictures of water in the upper and lower containers and put the pictures in order, showing an understanding of succession and order in time. Next, children understood that the drop in one container and the rise in the other took the same amount of time to occur; they could understand temporal intervals between succeeding temporal points. At the third stage, he found that children could understand that events can occur at the same time and also that temporal intervals can be added together. They then became able to measure time as a temporal unit. Piaget suggested that it was not until this stage had been reached that children could understand 'lived time', 'age' and internal subjective time.

If children cannot understand how long situations may last in relation to each other, or the sequence or coincidence of events, it was therefore often implied that history is not a suitable subject for young children. Peel (1967) concluded that young children cannot understand the nature of history or the significance of time within it. They may understand that William I became King, but not the implications of his reign or the place in historical time into which it fits.

Other researchers have considered the cultural, intellectual and philosophical implications of the concept of time, and asked how central this concept is to historical understanding. Jahoda (1963) said that conceptions of time and history depend on the social and intellectual climate; they are subjective. This approach had been illustrated in a study by Bernot and Blancard (1953). They showed how farm labourers in a French village, whose families had lived there for generations, had a perspective which went beyond their personal experience, whereas immigrant glass-blowers from itinerant families who moved into the village were almost without a sense of the past. People's different perspectives are clearly important in a local study. Children on a new suburban estate, or in an area with a large number of immigrants, will have different perspectives of the past from those in an isolated, long-established rural community.

The concept of time is cultural as well as subjective. The doings of Cromwell, the Act of Union, and the Famine of 1847 may seem more recent to an Irishman than to an Englishman. Teachers need to be increasingly aware of children's different personal and cultural narratives, given the enormous migration in the modern world. As Bruner has written recently,

> It is not easy, however multicultural your intentions, to help a ten-year-old create a story that includes him in the world beyond his family and neighbourhood, having been transplanted from Vietnam to the San Fernando Valley, from Algeria to Lyons, from Anatolia to Dresden.

And he warns that:

> If school, his *pied-à-terre* outside the family, can't help him there are alienated counter cultures that can.
>
> (Bruner 1996: 41)

Lello wondered whether, since time is not a natural and self-evident order, it really matters that an historical incident should be fixed in context and time. 'Is Herodotus devalued because his chronology is imaginary? Is Thucydides inferior because dates and chronology are almost ignored?' (1980: 344). Leach (1973) pointed out that the preoccupation of the early Christian authors with a numerical point of view was not in order to record dates, but because of their obsession with number logic. (This is seen, for example, in the representation of time, space and symbolism in The Westminster Pavement in Westminster Abbey.) If this view had not been abandoned, most modern development, especially science, could not have occurred. However, the implication of the change is that time is now inextricably linked with number in Western culture.

Lello concluded that chronology, though of undoubted importance, is not intrinsic to an understanding of time or history.

> Knowledge and a grasp of chronology are by no means synonymous with historical sense. Teaching history involves coming to terms with particular ways of explaining time to children which could, and sometimes does, run the risk of moulding children into preferred patterns of thinking, just as a rigid school timetable segments the day into artificial boxes.
>
> (Lello 1980: 347)

Friedman (1978) suggested that children of about four years old become aware of time through events specific to themselves and to people in their immediate surroundings; the past and the present are differentiated by words such as 'before' and 'after', 'now' and 'then'. Similarly, Piaget (1952) and Vygotsky (1962) showed how children gradually learn through trial and error to form sets of objects linked by a shared attribute; in the context of history as they make collections of 'now' and 'then', or 'old' and 'new', they try to explain their underlying reasons for the sets they form. Harpin (1976) like Piaget (1928) showed how growing maturity in children's syntax reflects their increasing ability to use conjunctions related to time and to cause and effect instead of 'and'. 'Autumn came and the leaves fell' becomes 'Because Autumn came, the leaves fell'. Harner (1982) showed that understanding these words depended on an understanding of the varied linguistic structures of the past tense and also of adverbs such as 'yesterday', 'before', 'last week' or 'already'. Thornton and Vukelich (1988) found that between four and six years old children began to order their daily routines chronologically from early morning until bed time, while Bradley (1947) had identified a third 'time distinction' beginning at six or seven years old when clock-time skills appear to develop from larger to smaller units (hour to minute to second) while calendar time appears to work in reverse (from days to weeks to months).

Nevertheless, Marbeau (1988) argued that children of six have a very narrow and discontinuous grasp of their own duration and that they build continuity into their existence by reciting it to others and to themselves. Yet he said that this did not impair their interest in the past because they are interested in 'the problem of origins'.

Smith and Tomlinson (1977) studied the understanding of historical duration of children between 8 and 15. Children were asked to construct two historical intervals from their own knowledge of historical persons and/or events, to make absolute and comparative judgement of their durations, and to provide a rationale for these judgements. First the child was asked to name an historical person or event, then to work backwards or forwards from this anchor point, in one direction at a time, providing a minimum of three items coming 'just before' or 'just after' that in order to define a subjective historical period. The researcher wrote the items on cards. The child was then asked, 'how long do you think that took in history – a very long time, a long time, not very long, a short time, a very short time?' The same process was repeated with respect to a second historical period, and the child was asked to compare the durations of the two intervals. S/he was asked to arrange the first set of cards in order. The second set was arranged beneath them by the researcher to cover the same distance, and the child was asked, 'Which of the two sets of historical items do you think took longest? How could you tell?' Analysis revealed a sequence of responses:

1. arbitrary;
2. those equating historical intervals with the number of items (well, er, there's more things happened);

3. those which related the duration to the number of items of a particular type (the longest was the one with the most kings and queens), or to the amount of activity (modern wars are over quicker. Look at the weapons);
4. a recognition of a need for an independent scale, such as calendar years;
5. the child is able to overlap synchronous and partially overlapping intervals, and consistently apply an equal interval scale.

The value of such a study is that, having recognised a sequence of development, teachers are able to focus more clearly on the stage of a child's understanding and so to accelerate it. West (1981) found that children have a great deal of information about the past which they have not learned in school, and this enables them to sequence artefacts and pictures quite competently.

Crowther (1982) investigated children's understanding of the dynamics of stability and change. He found that seven-year-olds regard change in terms of direct actions performed and as the substitution of one thing for another, taking little account of the time factor involved, but gradually children see change as part of the universal order of things, of transformation and gradual development, recognising succession and continuity in change, although they show less understanding of the disintegrating effects of change. As one 11-year-old said, 'Everything alters in different times and different ways. Change can be dramatic; it can come gradually and you hardly notice it at all'.

Complicated concepts of time then involve understanding the language of time, chronological sequences, duration, causes and effects over time, similarities and differences between past and present and the measurement of time. Research suggests the ways in which these understandings develop slowly and piecemeal through relating subjective experiences to different units of measurement of time. Gradually children build up their own maps of the past which constantly change as new information is added. It is a map children carry in their heads rather than a chronological map or a framework of facts.

An on-going large-scale research project is investigating how children, during Key Stages 2 and 3, build up these mental maps (Dickinson and Lee 1994). It began by tracing children's developing understanding of motive (why people in the past may have behaved as they did) and of cause and effect (why things happened). These two strands of the National Curriculum for History (chronological understanding and describing reasons for and results of historical events, situations and changes), may turn out not to be as closely related as is assumed. So far, clusters of ideas are emerging which are, to some extent, hierarchical, about children's ability to explain reasons for behaviour. They were asked to explain reasons for Anglo-Saxon trial by ordeal and for Claudius' invasion of Britain. Responses fell into one of the following categories – children would:

- repeat what happened but not attempt to explain it;
- explain the behaviour in their own terms and so not attempt to understand why it seemed 'stupid';
- think that people were not stupid but behaved as they did because 'they were not as clever as us';
- assume that people in the past were very much like people today;
- project themselves into the past in an attempt to understand the behaviour of people who were in a different situation from their own;
- recognise that they needed to change perspective to that of the other person's situation.

An adult, given the same tests, recognised that to understand the motives of people in the past it is necessary to set their behaviour in the wider context of different beliefs, values and material considerations – the ideas, beliefs, attitudes and experiences of men, women and children in the past.

The second aspect of the research investigates children's understanding of causes of events in the context of the Roman invasion of Britain, through three tests. In the first, the question is represented as a paradox: there were lots of Britons in Britain; the Roman army was not very big; the Britons were fighting for their homes. So why were the Romans able to take over most of Britain?

In the second test, the children were asked to draw as many arrows as they wished between boxes to assess their understanding of interconnecting factors of different levels of significance and interdependence. In the third test, two brief explanations were offered. One reflected the background to the issue (the Roman Empire was rich and ordered); the other described an event in the process of conquest (the Romans beat the British at the Battle of the Medway). Children were asked, 'How can you have two different explanations of the same thing?'

Since 1995 work on the CHATA project (Concepts of History and Teaching Approaches) (Lee *et al.* 1996 a, b, c, d) has shown that, in spite of assumptions that our history teaching is enquiry based most pupils in Year 3 and many in Years 6, 7 and 9 still think that all the answers can be found in books and that there is a simple, linear story of the past if only they can find it. They are reluctant to question the sources or seek further evidence. Yet the researchers recognise that this depends very much on teaching approaches. They found the ideas of some seven-year olds about explanation and the nature of historical knowledge to be as sophisticated as those of some 14-year-olds. Tom, in Year 3, explained that 'the fact that the Romans wanted tin and pearls from Britain' did not explain why they took over Britain 'cos, you see, just because they wanted them it doesn't mean that they're going to be able to take over' (Lee *et al.* 1998).

Stow (2000) found that young children's concepts of historical time have become much more developed since the introduction of the National Curriculum although this is uneven, depending more on the school and teaching strategies used than on age. He found that in 1998 able six-year olds could label periods and categorise pictures according to some periods (particularly Roman) and tackled with confidence an activity to identify and sequence pictures within a period. As recently as 1993, in Harnett's and Lynn's research studies, six-year olds had found this threatening. Stow found that the majority of eight- to nine-year-olds could label periods with confidence and understanding, place periods in the correct century, sequence them and were confident in describing the shared characteristics of the Tudor, Roman and World War II periods and those of the 1990s. Eleven-year-olds could recall accurately and use dates associated with a period; understanding of period seemed to develop more readily through codified, visual images than confidence in dates.

You do not have to be an academic researcher to analyse the reasoning that lies behind children's understanding, and also their misconceptions. Indeed all the research described in this chapter endorses the opportunities for students and teachers to do this as an integral part of their planning, teaching and evaluation and also the need to do so, in order to teach real history and accelerate children's thinking.

Student teachers investigate children's concepts of time

Katherine Hetherington planned a sequence of activities through which she hoped she would learn more about her Year 1 pupils' concepts of time: sequencing a combination of coloured and black and white photographs of paintings; family photographs across generations; sorting into sets of 'old' and 'new'; talking about personal memories. She analysed their responses and identified different levels of both understanding and misconception. Chris for example claimed that Katherine, in a sequence of her family photographs, could not be the same person: 'Don't be silly. She's different in each one', while Holly said 'they're obviously all you and your brother, who is older than you, from when you're a baby to now' and could explain the clues to the passing of time. Yet reasoning based on evidence in attempting to sequence photographs of elderly relatives did not always lead to the correct answer. Great-great-aunt did indeed look younger than gran!

Another group of students, asked to teach concepts of chronology to a Year 3 class, identified some of their common misconceptions. For example when asked to put each of the students' sequences of dated photographs of themselves on a 30-year time-line they found it difficult not to place them at equal intervals (Smith and Tomlinson 1977) and their assumption that large photographs indicated greater age, and that the tallest student was the oldest are pure Piaget! Piaget (1956) had found that a young child's notion of age often equated with size.

> Recognising and responding to pupils' misconceptions, awareness of recent classroom research and the ability to use it to inform and improve teaching are now requirements for the Award of Qualified Teacher Status (DfEE 1998b). Awareness of subject specific research makes it possible to identify and respond to children's existing understanding, and misunderstandings, to plan for progression, and to evaluate, modify and refine practice.
>
> (Huggins 2000)

Other historical concepts

Other researchers have investigated concepts loosely related to history. Not surprisingly, they traced three broad levels of development. Coltham (1960) chose 'king', 'early man', 'invasion', 'ruler', 'trade' and 'subject'. She asked children between 9 and 13 years old to draw what each concept conveyed to them, to choose the picture they thought conveyed the concept best from six pictures of each concept representing different levels of understanding, to define it verbally, and to choose appropriate doll's clothes to represent the concept. She found that at first, children depended on visual information and personal experience; later they were able to coordinate different points of view with their own experience, and at the highest level they showed awareness that concepts change with time.

Da Silva (1969) gave children a passage in which 'slum' was recorded as a nonsense word and asked them what they thought this nonsense word meant. At the lowest level, he found no attempt to use clues in the text, then a logically constructed response although the meaning changed with the context, and finally a level of deductive conceptualisation, when each piece of evidence was weighed against the others, and a stable definition for the nonsense word was achieved.

Booth (1979) asked secondary school children to group pictures and quotations related to 'Imperialism' and 'Nationalism' and classified their responses as concrete if the groups were based on physical facts in the evidence, such as colour of skin and abstract if they inferred relationships. He found responses were influenced by good teaching, interest and parental involvement. Furth (1980) also postulated landmarks in the development of children's understanding of the social world. He asked children between 5 and 11 questions about social roles, money, government and communities. Their answers indicated a growing understanding of these concepts, from seeing society as unrelated individuals, to a grasp of a concrete, systematic framework at 11. He showed, for example, that at five, the primary cause for taking on a role is seen as a personal wish, but between five and seven, children stress the notion of order, and by 11 they focus on the idea of succession ('I suppose if someone leaves, someone comes') and the expertise inherent in a role ('Nearly every job you do, there has to be a man in charge'). Similarly, with government, children first had an image of a special man, then of a ruler, then of a job-giver or owner of land, until at nine or ten they understood that a government provides function and services in return for taxes.

Research, then, has shown how concepts develop through a process of generalisation, by storing an image of abstracted characteristics, and of deduction, by drawing from the stored image, adding to it and modifying it. It has indicated a pattern in the development of concepts, suggested that concepts need to be taught, and that they are best learned through discussion.

Research has also shown that children who are encouraged to become involved in applying their knowledge about the past, to discuss, make and support judgements, reach decisions, make connections with charts and diagrams, are enabled to extend their vocabulary and develop abstract historical concepts (Husbands 1996: 15, 27). And this in turn enables them to go beyond the specific to the general, to abstract from the detail the wider issues, to make links and connections across time, and between past and present (Hunt 2000). Sampson *et al.* (1998) have recently studied the ways in which teachers intervene to develop children's subject-specific language and concepts in history.

Note 9 on the Romans, Anglo-Saxons and Vikings in Britain, National Curriculum Study Unit (DfEE 1999b: 106) suggests how significant concepts could be traced across this period (government and religion, settlement, farming, social structure and trade) and studied in depth in relation to significant events and people of one particular group. These concepts could well be the focus of links across all the study units.

The revised curriculum also stresses the importance of learning to use language across the curriculum and states in particular that pupils should be taught the specialist vocabulary of each subject and also to use the procedural concepts of a subject in order to learn and ask and answer questions and to develop arguments. Examples given incude causality, chronology, hypothesis and comparison.

Chapter 3

The Implementation of the Revised National Curriculum for History 2000: A Whole-School Approach

The rationale for the revised (2000) curriculum claims firstly an enhanced emphasis on flexibility and relevance: in responding to pupils' individual differences, strengths, interests, experiences; to their special educational needs; to local priorities. Secondly it emphasises the importance of English, mathematics and Information and Communications Technology in developing the thinking processes central to each subject across a broadly based, coherent and progressive curriculum. The generic introduction (DfEE 1999b: 10–13; 19–23) talks about working together with families and the local community, in rich and varied contexts, to develop enquiring minds, able to think rationally, creatively, critically, and to develop a sense of identity through knowledge and understanding of spiritual, moral, social and cultural heritages, in local, national, European and international dimensions. It is expected that key skills are embedded in all the subjects of the National Curriculum: skills of communication, social skills, enquiry skills, creative thinking and awareness of the processes of learning in each subject. Suggestions for ways in which key skills can be developed through history are given in QCA/DfEE 2000 (pp. 9–11).

The programme of study for history identifies its distinctive contribution as engaging with the past through critical enquiry in order to understand cultural diversity and in this context to clarify personal choices, attitudes and values. (There seems to be a real danger which we need to guard against in this value-laden rationale, of young children judging the past by the knowledge-base, values and attitudes of the present.)

However, there are also real opportunities for exciting history education. This depends on creating thoughtful schemes of work. A scheme of work is defined as 'overall planned provision for history in a school. It includes both key stage plans and units of work' (QCA/DfEE 1998b; 2000). Issue 26 of *Primary History*, a special extended edition, focused on helping teachers to implement the revised order through developing manageable schemes of work.

Areas for professional judgement: planning a scheme of work

In order to use the framework of the Revised National Curriculum as a basis for designing a coherent curriculum which reflects the needs of their own school, teachers need to make judgements about balance, breadth, depth and progression. This involves decisions about the structure of the curriculum, the selection of areas of study and the ways in which they are linked horizontally to other areas of the curriculum and vertically to each other. All the staff need to participate in making these decisions, although the leadership role of the coordinator is crucial. OFSTED (1999) found that in many schools, subject leaders see their role as providers of ideas and resources, rather than helping colleagues to develop and evaluate schemes. Lomas (1994) gave a good overview of the ways in which a history coordinator can support colleagues in devising an effective, whole-school programme. This has been further developed by Davies and Redmond (1998).

The structure of the curriculum

It now seems essential, given the emphasis on developing literacy, numeracy and ICT skills, that if the skills of historical enquiry are to continue to be learned in meaningful and enjoyable contexts, these are linked in some ways to other curriculum areas. There are also good pedagogical reasons for recognising links between history and other subjects. History is an umbrella discipline; it involves all aspects of the life of a society – its art, music, science, technology, religion. It lies at the core of the humanities and involves children's emotional and social as well as cognitive development. Language, mathematics and ICT are systems of communication which are required to be taught in purposeful contexts and an historical investigation is one very suitable such context.

It also seems reasonable that units of work in history should be taught as blocked work, at specified times during each year. Curriculum balance does not derive from equal distribution across all points at all times. SCAA (1995) defined blocked work as drawn from a single subject focusing on a distinct and cohesive body of knowledge, understanding and skills, and taught over a specific period of time, which has the potential for linking with units of work in other subjects.

Identifying the nature of the links is crucial in order to identify the key learning objective of an activity and retain the distinct content and processes of enquiry of each subject. It may be a number of subjects, linked through a theme; a local study involving history, geography, science and art, for example. It may be that the subjects are linked by content, but the skills and concepts to be learned are linked only to one subject; a model of a Tudor house may support a history topic but teach concepts of shape and space and measuring skills. Sometimes it is possible to teach learning objectives for history concurrently with requirements of the literacy, or numeracy framework, or the ICT curriculum. Examples are given in the *History Teacher's Guide* (QCA/DfEE 1998b); others are explored in Chapter 5. Suggestions for contexts in which links between history and other subjects can be teased out were given in previous editions; arguably these are more valid than ever and so are included in this edition to indicate starting points for developing cross-curricular links.

I   *Mathematics*
(i)   *Shape and space*
Properties of two-dimensional shapes:
identify shapes in buildings: windows, doors, pediments.
Properties of three-dimensional shapes:
identify cuboids, cubes (buildings, steps), prisms (roofs), cylinders (pillars, chimneys); measure, reduce to scale, make nets and models of buildings.
Maps, journeys, plans of sites.

(ii)   *Number/algebra/symmetry*
Repeating patterns: windows, railings, terraces.
Tesellations: brickwork, tiles, mosaics, garden design, wallpaper, fabric.

(iii)   *Measures. Length/distance*
Measure routes (scale).
Time, speed and distance calculations.
Measure buildings.
Record size (e.g. of ships) by drawing on ground.

Time.
Time zones, devices for calculating solar time.
Different ways of measuring time (sand clocks, water clocks, candle clocks).
Different ways of recording time (Chinese, Indian, Arabic, European calendars), agricultural calendars, ships' logs, school and factory time-tables, diaries. Changing attitudes to and effects of precise measurement of time.

Weight
Recipes, rations, diet. Weight of load carried (e.g. coal carried by child labourer). Weight of cattle and sheep at beginning and end of eighteenth century.
Capacity (e.g. how much beer drunk daily at Hampton Court in reign of Henry VIII).

Money
Price of food, proportion of income.

(iv) *Number calculations and estimations, data collection, presentation and interpretation*
Statistics
Census returns.
Street directories.
Graveyard studies.
Parish records.
Population statistics.
Trade figures.
Questionnaires and surveys.

Time-lines
Counting systems in other cultures
Information about journeys can often be found in diaries, letters and oral accounts, advertisements for stage coaches, newspapers and old time-tables. Statistics about trade or population figures can be extracted from books written for adults. Calculations can be used to investigate historical questions.

II *Language*
(i) *Speaking and listening*
Discussion of evidence, using selected concepts (how was it made, how does it work, what does it tell us about the past, is it a reliable source? Supporting points of view with argument).
Interviews and questionnaires.
Listening to fiction about the past, listening to stories, myths, legends, accounts.
Presenting findings as slide shows or on video or oral tape, or directly to audiences of children, parents or other members of the community.
Discussion of how to interpret evidence (e.g. while modelmaking, drawing).
'Home corner' play using old artefacts.
Drama, role-play, debate (did the Ancient Greeks treat women fairly?), improvising stories, puppet plays, 'hot-seating' (what would you do next?), freeze-frames based on a picture (who are you? what are you doing?).
Listening to video or oral tape-recordings.

(ii) *Reading*

Reading visual images (films, books, photographs).

Making books, brochures, posters to present findings (individual, group or class).

Reading stories about the past (consider viewpoints, motives, how true the story may be).

(iii) *Writing*

Note-taking from teacher's presentation: from reference books. Labels to explain what models, drawings, historical sources, tell us about the past (e.g. in a class museum).

Quizzes about evidence (e.g. a museum trail).

Letters (e.g. to museums and galleries or to invite visitors to the school).

Directions (e.g. for other visitors to a site or gallery).

Stories, plays, poems, based on evidence, describing and explaining the past.

Writing presenting a point of view (how true is this diary account?).

Reviews of stories about the past.

Shared writing (e.g. working in groups to write newspapers from different viewpoints).

Writing about science investigations connected with history topic.

III *Science*

(i) *Materials*

Used to make toys, buildings, transport, clothes, tools and machines; what are their properties, where do they come from, how have they changed, why?

(ii) *Processes of life*

Health, hygiene, diet, medicines, now and in the past.

How have they changed? Why? What have been the effects of changes?

(iii) *Genetics and evolution*

Selective growth of crops and breeding of domestic animals; changes in food and farming.

(iv) *Earth and atmosphere*

Influences of climate, rainfall, wind direction, soil-type on settlement.

(v) *Forces*

Tools, machines, transport, buildings.

(vi) *Electricity and Information Technology*

Effects on daily life (e.g. of domestic appliances).

(vii) *Energy*

Toys; how do they work?

Wind, water, steam, nuclear power; effects on way of life, causes and effects of change.

(viii) *Sound and music*

Musical instruments in the past; how did they work? Music, what did it sound like, who played/listened; when? Song, dance.

(ix) *Light*

Scientific revolution: lenses, telescopes, new ideas about the earth in space.

IV   *Art*

Study of contemporary paintings and design.

Observational drawing, developed in other media: painting, printing, embroidery.

Design based on detail in fabric, ceramics, furniture, or in building materials (wood, brick, stone, iron). (Printing, computing.)

Modelmaking in junk, balsa wood (e.g. timber-frame building), pottery, in order to reconstruct an artefact, building, street or site from available evidence.

V   *Technology*

Modelmaking; making 'props' for role-play or for class museum, or for acting out a story; grinding seeds, making dough, cooking recipes from period; carding, spinning, weaving, dying wool; drawing plans of artefacts, or buildings, using simple machines or tools from the past (e.g. candle snuffer, button hook); copying old designs in fabric, needlework, wallpaper, mosaics, pottery.

VI   *Geography*

(i)   Making and reading maps.

(ii) Understanding places, reasons for settlement; climate, relief, resources.

(iii) Communication between settlements; social, economic, aesthetic.

(iv) Reasons for changes in settlements or populations.

VII *Religious education*

Belief systems, celebration of beliefs (places of worship and festivals), effects of beliefs on individuals and communities.

After some general principles have been agreed on how subjects are to relate to each other, further questions need to be considered. How is teachers' subject expertise to be developed? What is the relationship between the Foundation Stage from Nursery to Year One, set out in the *Early Learning Goals* (QCA 1999), and the Key Stage 1 curriculum? How will history be` planned to provide effective learning opportunities for all pupils, including those with special educational needs? How can parents and the local community be involved? What gender issues do we need to address?

Developing subject expertise

The 1995 Report of the Chief Inspector for schools suggested that at Key Stage 2 teachers' subject knowledge, and therefore curriculum planning and assessment, was generally seen to be inadequate. Since then history has fared badly in terms of professional development opportunities (OFSTED 1999). Therefore in some schools, children at the top of Key Stage 2 are taught by more than one teacher in order to share teachers' curriculum strengths. Is this desirable in your school? What might be the advantages, alternatives?

Progression from Nursery to Key Stage 1

There are many opportunities to identify links between the 6 areas of learning set out in the *Early Learning Goals* (QCA 1999) and history in Key Stage 1, particularly in the areas of personal, social and emotional development, language and literacy and knowledge and understanding of the world. It is possible to develop concepts of time, interpretation and inference in the context of changes in family life, the environment and stories.

Time

Children can explore sequence and the passing of time in relation to their family history through such stories as *Once There Were Giants* (Waddell and Dale 1989), through talking about family photographs and listening to the 'true stories' of older people. Through shared reading they can learn to repeat and retell sequences of events, follow a plot, create images which they have not experienced in sensory reality (cinders, city gates, pump). They enjoy new vocabulary. They learn to ask questions, make predictions, learn grammatical structures (if…then; because). Children between two and three can learn about cause and effect, motives and rules through predictable stories, *Rosie's Walk* (Hutchins 1973) or *Peter Rabbit* (who ignores the advice not to go into Mr McGregor's Garden with predictable consequences). The Billy Goats Gruff go up the hill 'to get fat'. Between four and five years of age children begin to see things from points of view other than their own and to develop insights about people. This is a good basis for talking about why people in the past did things, why events happened, for sequencing photographs, objects, events, comparing similarities and differences and using more precise time vocabulary at Key Stage 1.

Interpretations

Young children can begin to understand different interpretations. Thomas (1993) found that nursery-age children were able to discuss meanings in pictures which were explicitly different from the text (e.g. *Never Satisfied*, Testa 1982). They can compare traditional versions of fairy stories with modern interpretations, or compare different illustrations. They can create interpretations through play. Moyles (1989) suggested that play in the context of a pretend castle, an old kitchen, a Victorian classroom for dolls or a palace helps children both to understand themselves and their self-worth, and also to explore what it might have been like to be somebody else.

Historical sources

Decoding pictures, book illustrations, paintings; photographs, can provide a good starting point for making inferences about historical sources. Children first learn to talk about the ideas, moods and feelings they represent, and infer from facial expressions and body language what people may be thinking, feeling or saying. Old illustrations, for example in Kate Greenaway or Beatrix Potter books, are themselves historical sources. Suggestions for activities linking Foundation Stage and Key Stage 1 history are given in Cooper (1995b) and overarching guidance in the *History Teacher's Guide* (QCA/DfEE 1998b).

Responding to diverse learning needs

History can be an ideal subject for adapting to meet the diverse needs of pupils, from a variety of social and cultural backgrounds, different ethnic groups and linguistic backgrounds, and those with a range of special educational needs or disabilities. The sources of history are richly varied: musical, visual, tactile. History can be explored through stories, oral sources, role-play, drama reconstructions and simulations, CD Roms and videos. Findings can be presented through photographs, ICT, role-play, models, paintings. One example of such an adaptation was made by sighted children for a group of partially sighted friends. They made a tactile plan of their local church, and an audio recording of supporting information, then accompanied their friends on a visit to the church and asked them to evaluate their model and tape. A rich experience for everyone – and they also learned a lot about writing literacy hour instructional text! Another moving example of work on the Victorians carried out by Margaret Taylor, a trainee teacher placed in a school for children with severe learning difficulties, is given in Cooper (1995b: 169–81). Sebba (1994) gives many further suggestions for supporting children with special educational needs through history.

Involving parents and the community

The revised curriculum re-emphasises the importance of working with parents and of making links between work in school and the community. History offers rich opportunities, through local history (changes in the community and key events, studied through buildings, memorials, work-places, oral sources), through family history; by involving parents and other adults in out-of-school visits and preparation and follow up work in school; in presenting findings of enquiries in local libraries, baby clinics, old people's homes and other public places, or in the local newspaper. David (1996) describes a project in which parents and children and teachers work together on history projects.

Raising awareness of gender issues

Recent studies (e.g. Hayes: QCA 1998; Sukhnandan *et al.* 2000) have suggested that boys' reading and writing skills lag behind those of girls. History is dependent on spoken language, but enquiries and presentations are not necessarily dependent on extended reading or writing. It is however interesting that the new emphasis on accessing and creating non-fiction text is proving very attractive to boys: it seems that boys enjoy the opportunities provided by the literacy framework for finding out from information books, and reading and creating information text: diagrams, plans, instructions, using notes, captions, labels; using writing frames to develop arguments, or explanations. History can maximise these opportunities.

On the other hand, it is important to recognise that some aspects of areas of study in history may be more interesting to either boys or girls and to allow for these possibilities. It is also important to be aware that women are still seriously under-represented in sources in school books and when they do show women the sources are rarely interpreted from a female point of view (Pounce 1995). Osler (1995) suggests that teachers are careful to acknowledge great women alongside the men of the past, and encourage children to study the experiences of 'ordinary women'; children should consider why women have been invisible and undervalued; discuss how they are portrayed.

The revised curriculum makes it explicit that the interests and concerns of boys and girls should be taken into account by using a range of activities and contexts for work and by avoiding gender stereotyping.

Long-term planning: selecting and sequencing areas of study

A long-term plan is defined in the *History Teacher's Guide* (QCA/DfEE 1998b) as one which shows how teaching units are distributed across the years of both key stages in a sequence that promotes both curriculum continuity and progression in children's learning. Units may be linked with work in other subjects. This document provides a good model for identifying a sequence of units of investigation for Years 1–6 derived from the National Curriculum Programmes of Study, with approximate time allocations. A matrix (QCA/DfEE 2000: 13–15) maps these investigations to show how they reflect the areas of study, key elements of skills, knowledge and understanding, and breadth and depth and other perspectives and dimensions. However it is intended that if this model is used it is modified, both in terms of the units of investigation and the focuses within them. The Historical Association, in its response to the consultation, warned that the exemplar names given in the National Curriculum could distort history teaching and confuse teachers, focusing as they do on white, Anglo-Saxon, male history. It also stressed the importance of giving prominence to local history, as an aspect of other areas of study. It emphasised the need to make a reality the stated encouragement to stimulate pupils' curiosity, to work closely with providers of history beyond the classroom such as museums and sites; to make links between history, and literacy, numeracy, ICT and citizenship, and the need to ensure we focus on the affective side of history, on imagination and the ways in which people in the past may have felt (Lomas 1999).

Deciding on units of investigation

In deciding on titles for their own units of investigation (the most creative and exciting though more time-consuming approach) or modifying those given, teachers need first to brainstorm resources within their own locality: museums, art galleries, sites and buildings related to the British areas of study; significant local events, industries, and work-places, people, periods of significant change. What may link most closely to the interests and experiences and personal histories of the children and their families?

Having listed resources in the locality, other resources the school has already acquired and the interests and needs of pupils, it is possible to outline four or five units of study for Key Stage 1, which include the recent and more distant past, significant men, women and children and events, both in Britain and the wider world. At Key Stage 2 decisions can be made about which of the British areas of study to focus on (Romans, Anglo-Saxons or Vikings; Victorian Britain or Britain since 1930); which links best with a 'local study'. Britain and the wider world in Tudor times and a European study of Ancient Greece are not optional. Which ancient world study is to be selected (Ancient Egypt, Sumer, the Assyrian Empire, the Indus Valley, the Maya, Benin or the Aztecs)? Are there cultural links with the local community or links with a geography topic? Drawing on resources and previous experience it is then possible to decide on questions to investigate within each area of study and which aspects of knowledge, skills and understanding to focus on in each study. Pupils and parents could be involved in this process, evaluating what they had found most interesting in studying these units in the past, and making suggestions for new enquiries, and activities in future.

Sequencing investigations

How then should the units of enquiry be sequenced? There is no firm evidence that children develop a concept of time or chronology through chronologically sequenced topics. It seems more likely that cross-referencing between periods and devising time-lines of different calibrations is more challenging in structuring mental maps across study units. And the thinking processes of a discipline identified in the programmes of study, if translated into appropriate forms, can be grappled with by pupils of any age (Bruner 1966).

Progression in thinking is developed through the design of the units; this is discussed in Chapter 4. A rationale for sequencing the units may evolve through considering a series of questions.

- Are the central questions and related sources for some investigations intrinsically more intellectually demanding or sensitive than others?
- Do some units involve longer journeys appropriate for older children?
- Is there an overarching question which runs through several units (e.g. why did people move to new lands)? This would allow comparison over a long period of time. For example, a local study might reflect a key economic focus within the community; farming, a port or a key industry such as mining or textiles; there could be a focus on changes in farming or in cloth production through Saxon, Tudor and Victorian times; the changing significance of a port could be traced from a Saxon settlement, through Tudor exploration to Victorian trade in the nineteenth century or a seaside resort in the twentieth. This would encompass changes over a long period of time and also develop economic and industrial awareness.
- Is it best at Key Stage 1 to study a period linked to a Key Stage 2 topic, or to study a topic (e.g. castles) because this is not a focus in Key Stage 2?
- Is it possible to design bridging units which span Foundation–Y1 and Y2–Y3?
- Can links be made across key stages e.g. KS1/KS2: Myths and legends from an ancient civilisation (KS1) – related non-European unit (KS2); local study (KS1) – local study (KS2); famous person or event (KS1) – related study unit (KS2). KS2/KS3: local study (KS2) – Britain 1066–1500 (KS3); Tudors (KS2 Year 6) – Britain 1066–1500 (KS3)?
- Can a non-European and a British study unit be linked, e.g. Benin/Victorian Britain or Tudors? (A past non-European society could be linked with Britain since 1930 and the growth of a multicultural society.) Links could be traced between Ancient Egypt and Ancient Greece.

- Is it possible to identify key concepts which run through all societies over a sequence of study units; for example government (rules, who makes and enforces them and why); culture (art, music, literature, architecture); social (people and how they related to each other); communication (within and between societies)? This approach would:
    (i)   encourage coherence and continuity by identifying key concepts and encouraging comparison between then and now and between areas of study;
    (ii) encourage progression as concepts are understood in increasingly complex ways (Vygotsky 1962);
    (iii) enable pupils to transfer what they have learned, to extrapolate from particular memorable instances to the general in order to transfer skills learned to other similar problems, gaining confidence and avoiding mental overload (Bruner 1966);
    (iv) encourage pupils to make connections, understand significance and relevance and avoid the notion of 'one damn thing after another'.
- Are there fixed points in the school's long-term plan where history can be linked to other subjects? For example can links be made with geography units (Egypt/Greece; Tudors/Aztecs/Central America; Asia/Indus Valley; Africa/Benin)? Are there opportunities for links with religious education, music, technology or art curricula?

In mixed age classes, history needs to be planned in cycles over time which provide opportunities for progression through the key elements, key skills and key concepts at appropriate levels and avoid duplicating content.

Having decided on the sequence of units of enquiry the school rationale needs to state how each unit builds on and refers to, revisits, or reinforces similar or related aspects of history; builds on children's prior experiences, conceptual knowledge, existing skills and understanding; moves from personal historical knowledge, to a wider range of areas and the links between them. This constitutes the whole-school long-term plan.

However, progression in children's thinking is planned for in detail through the learning objectives in the medium-term plans. These are discussed in Chapter 4.

Chapter 4

Case Studies: Medium-Term Plans and Examples of Work

The medium-term plans in this chapter are examples of units of work, developed from the whole-school and key stage plans. They set out the learning objectives, teaching activities and opportunities for assessing differentiated learning outcomes across two or three of the levels described in the history attainment target. This structure reflects that of the exemplar units (QCA/DfEE 1998b) in which the learning outcomes are intended to be appropriate for most of the children in units planned for Year 1 or Year 2, and for children across two year groups at Key Stage 2 (Y3/4 or Y5/6), with modifications for those who make less or more progress. This welcome broad brushstrokes approach to monitoring progression in history recognises that development in historical thinking is complex because of the number of variables involved, depending on the questions asked, the sources and activities selected, the kinds of responses expected. It therefore also recognises the central role of the teachers in planning, monitoring, modifying and reviewing work to meet the needs and interests of the children in their classes.

The exemplar units (QCA/DfEE 1998b) also reflect research into the importance of teaching selected key vocabulary: concepts related to the period, created by historians (Anglo-Saxon, Blitz); words peculiar to a period (hypocaust, timber-framed), abstract vocabulary central to understanding societies and class (settlement, urbanisation, immigration) and concepts of time. In these units the teaching activities are presented as questions to investigate, rather than 'what I want the children to do' as in the medium-term plans given in this chapter. However this is a useful transposition; the skill in teaching is always for the children to think an investigation was all their own idea, and so within the constraints of what you want them to learn, to give them some real choices about the kinds of questions they want to ask.

Cross-curricular links

The webs showing how focuses within a history unit can be linked to other curricular areas are retained in this edition. Indeed they seem more relevant than ever in establishing the status of history within an integrated curriculum.

Examples of children's work arising from the plans in this chapter illustrate such links. Some activities have discrete history learning objectives making inferences about personal time-lines, family trees, artefacts (Greek vase paintings), about events (the Armada), or about stories (the *Odyssey*). Others are made meaningful by integration with the historical content but have learning objects in mathematics, science or English.

Some history units link particularly well with other dimensions of the curriculum. It may be useful (through whole-staff discussion) to identify particular opportunities to promote spiritual, moral, social or cultural development, citizenship or personal, social or health education in a 'points to note' column on each unit plan. These could then become part of an integrated whole-school plan. Opportunities for creative links are infinite and could generate lively staff discussion, making the rhetoric about flexibility in responding to children's interests and localities a reality. Some starting points for such discussion are given in QCA/DfEE 2000 (pp. 7–9).

A three-day history project in which trainee teachers and Key Stage 1 children, their teacher and the college tutor visited a local church indicates such opportunities (Cooper and Etches 1996). The work focused on history activities to develop concepts of change and continuity over time, through linking children's family history to historical sources found in a local church: pictures in windows, the font, family coats of arms, memorial stones and brasses, commemorative plaques from two world wars, poppy wreaths. Religious education, concepts of social and moral responsibility, community involvement, conflict and social, moral and cultural dimensions were inherent in this topic. What do the coats of arms stand for? Why? Can you find a poppy like this in the church? Who died? Why? Activities included role-play of baptisms and weddings, rubbings of brasses and memorial stones, designing new church windows, making family trees and oral history interviews as investigative reporters. Opportunities to make explicit the potential links between history and the frameworks for the PSHE and citizenship are given in QCA/DfEE 2000 (pp. 7–9).

Many aspects of the knowledge, skills and understandings set out in the non-statutory guidelines for personal, social and citizenship educaton (DfEE 1999b: 136–41) inevitably permeate good history teaching, which involves discussing incomplete sources, comparing accounts and interpretations, rooted in local and family history. At Key Stage 1 children are expected to work cooperatively, to take part in discussions, to share opinions, explain their views and listen to those of others; to understand that they belong to families, groups and communities; to meet and talk with other people; identify and respect differences between people; to understand the processes and changing needs of growing old. At Key Stage 2, in addition, they should reflect with imagination on social, moral, spiritual and cultural issues, understand other people's experiences and points of view and think about the lives of people living in other places and times, and people with different values and customs, consider social and moral dilemmas. What splendid opportunities for creative and lively history!

Grant Bage (1999) gives many examples of how real history can be taught through a variety of types of story about the past, and how such stories can also be used to promote spiritual, moral, social and cultural development. Stories, he says, can: transform children and teachers by altering understandings and behaviours; can explain and moralise; induct children into societies of the past and improve understanding of belief systems; describe and analyse human motivations; value local cultures and ideas while opening them to comparison and scrutiny. He shows how this can be done through teaching history.

Claire (1996) shows through practical examples how stories about the past can be used to promote the ethics of equality and diversity in creative and critical ways. Sherwood (1997) shows ways in which children can learn about cultural diversity as an integral part of all the Key Stage 2 areas of study, and Newman and Turpin (1997) have described how they taught the Roman unit to a Year 4 class from a rich diversity of cultural and religion backgrounds, through creating role-play based on investigation of the Roman spice trade.

Sarra Thorne, a Year 4 BA (QTS) history specialist student in 1999 investigated the ways in which OFSTED inspectors perceived social, moral, spiritual and cultural education being promoted through history lessons. She analysed inspection reports on a representative sample of 20 Cumbria primary schools. (OFSTED Homepage, http://www.ofsted.gov.uk/.) Sarra's analysis is given in Figure 4.1.

Evaluating progression in medium-term plans

One way of ensuring that a scheme of work reflects progression in the key aspects of historical enquiry from the goals for learning (QCA 1999) through the programmes of study from Key Stages 1 to 3, is to track these on a matrix and evaluate the learning objectives and teaching activities of the sequence of study units. A synopsis of such a matrix is given in Figure 4.2. This could inform the notes on required prior learning and expected outcomes for each unit. Other checklists for evaluating progression are given in QCA/DfEE 1998b (pp. 19–20).

	Aspects of history being taught	How are the history lessons promoting pupils' SMSC development?	History PoS or Key Elements
SOCIAL	– Older pupils know that they can find out about the past by… asking their parents and grandparents. – The school regularly asks older citizens about days gone by. – By the age of 7, pupils know famous people and their contribution to social development. – Recent work on the Second World War involved pupils talking with members of the local community about their war time experiences.	– School encouraging pupils to relate effectively with others. – Citizenship. – School encouraging pupils to participate in the community.	**Key Element 4** – Finding out about the past through adults talking about their own past. **Key Stage 1** – Area of Study 2 – Pupils should be taught about the lives of different kinds of famous men and women. **Study Unit 3b.** Britain since 1930 – Britons at war.
MORAL	– They knew something of the stories of Grace Darling and Guy Fawkes. – Pupils recognise there are reasons why people in the past acted as they did, e.g. pupils were able to discuss Guy Fawkes and his actions. – A study of the journey of Grace Darlington considering the view points involved. – Displays in classrooms include high quality artefact collections which pupils treat with care and respect.	– Providing pupils with opportunity to express moral values.	**Key Stage 1** – Area of Study 2. (As above) **Key Element 1** – Using artefacts – put in chronological order. **Key Element 4** – Historical enquiry – use artefacts to find out about aspects of the past.
SPIRITUAL	– A study of the journey of Grace Darling. – Visit to York Minster to experience atmosphere. – Year 6 visit to local church.	– Gain understanding on reflection of other peoples' beliefs. – Opportunity for reflection – awe and wonder.	**Key Element 4** – Finding out about aspects of the periods studied from buildings and site.
CULTURAL	– Pupils wrote briefly about why we wear poppies. – They know something of the history of the local lighthouse. – They have used the school Log Book to find first-hand evidence of the opening of the school in 1940. – Year 6 visit to local church. – Upper KS2 pupils are learning about historical development of Carlisle. – The pupils in Y1 make good progress in learning about their own personal history when completing own time-lines. – At KS1 they begin to learn about chronology by learning about recent events within their own families and in the community. – At KS2 pupils extend their understanding of chronology… learning includes key facts about local history. – Visits to museums and historic buildings linked to their studies also help to broaden their horizons. – Attainment in history is enhanced by the good use made of the historic setting of the school. – The school organises visits to places of historical interest to deepen pupils' insight and understanding.	– Developing knowledge of the nature and roots of their own cultural traditions. – Have a sense of their own identity and belonging within and have value for local, regional and national cultures. – Positive contributions made to pupils' cultural development through visits to museums and other historic sites.	**Key Stage 2** – Study Unit 3b, Britain since 1930. **Key Stage 2** – Study Unit 5, Local History. **Key Stage 2** – Britain since 1930. **Key Stage 1** – Area of Study 3 – notable and local events. **Key Element 1** – Chronology – time-line. **Key Stage 1** – Area of Study 1a – changes in their own lives and those of their family or those around them. **Key Element 4** – historical enquiry.

Figure 4.1 A synopsis of the references made to history activities which will also contribute to the development of pupils' social, moral, spiritual and cultural development. The references were made in the section on History in the OFSTED inspection reports

UNDERSTANDING	NURSERY-RECEPTION	KEY STAGE 1	KEY STAGE 2	KEY STAGE 3
Areas of Study	• family • locality • artefacts • events • perspectives	• lives and lifestyles of people in the recent past • famous people and events from the more distant past • use variety of sources	• four specified dimensions: local, national, Europe, global • coherence within a period: impact of personalities and events on everyday lives of men, women, children	• four dimensions integrated: locality, Britain, interacting with Europe and global contexts
Chronology, time concepts; cause/effect motive; similarity/difference	• sequence objects • talk and ask questions about changes over time	• sequence events and objects • use time vocabulary to identify differences; give reasons for causes, effects, motives	• sequence using appropriate periods • use vocabulary of time measurement to identify characteristics of periods, using specific characteristics, explain changes	• uses dates and specialised terms to describe changes over time • analyse and explain relationships between periods, recognising trends and patterns
Historical Interpretation		• identify different ways in which the past is represented	• identify different ways in which the past has been represented and subsequently interpreted	• know how and why historical events, people, situations and changes have been interpreted differently • evaluate interpretations
Historical Enquiry	• ask questions to gain information about why things happen; how things work; re family, locality, objects	• ask and answer questions about a greater range of sources (e.g. pictures, photographs, eye-witness accounts, ICT)	• select and record sources relevant to a focused enquiry; additional sources: documents, printed sources, music, sites, records	• evaluate sources; reach conclusions • use range of out of school sites, additional sources: oral, media
Organising and Communication Information	• recall in talking	• increased means of recall (e.g. writing, drawing, ICT)	• select information • use historical vocabulary	• prioritise information • use historical, chronological conventions • more emphasis on structure and explanation

Figure 4.2 Synpopsis of progression in history from the Foundation Stage to Key Stage 3

Key features are increasing complexity in: asking and answering questions; making links with other areas of learning and appreciating relevance in concepts; in explanations; in the ability to recognise categories, patterns, priorities of importance, and the judgements informed by an increasing range and depth of historical knowledge.

In evaluating the sequence of medium-term plans it may also be salutary to focus particularly on opportunities provided for considering different interpretations of one period in a subsequent period; to discriminate between and combine sources; to undertake open-ended investigations. These were the areas found to be weakest in 1994–98 OFSTED reports (OFSTED 1999).

Some recently published books provide irresistible opportunities for comparing interpretations of the past. Tony Robinson (1999) in *Kings and Queens* asks children to question the concept of historical truth, through anecdotes about, for example, Henry VIII's diseases and bad breath; Geraldine McCaughrean in *Britannia: 100 Great Stories from British History* (1999) points out that many of the stories she tells are myth, propaganda and 'downright lies' although they were once paraded as history, and although debunked as historic fact still have a place in our heritage.

And what about nursery rhymes as a means of describing the past while hiding comments and complaints in times when people could be hung, drawn and quartered for political comment (Ellerington 1997). It was Jack Horner who was asked by the Abbot of Glastonbury to deliver a pie to Henry VIII which contained the deeds of the abbey in an attempt to avoid its dissolution, but on the way he picked out the plum and the manor of Mells for himself. There are echoes of Sing-a-Song of Sixpence here too. Then there was Goosey Goosey Gander, the Bishop Gardner of Winchester, who could not find a way of arranging Henry VIII's divorce from Catherine of Aragon without upsetting her family in Spain and the Catholic church. But there is more about history and literacy in Chapter 5.

Plans for a local study at Key Stage 1 and at Key Stage 2

Figures 4.3 and 4.4 on pages 52 and 53 show how a local history study (which could link with local geography) might be developed in increasingly complex ways across Key Stages 1 and 2 through the sources used, the questions asked of them and the ways in which they are presented. Children at either stage can present their findings to audiences within and beyond the school in all sorts of ways and such presentations can be used as assessment opportunities. Activities in both figures reflect all of the key elements which can be structured to reflect a range of levels. Presentations might include slide shows, video and audio tapes, drama and role-play (developed from a home-corner reconstruction of an old kitchen, for example), story-telling, a museum exhibition or 'stalls' representing the researches of each group (maybe led by a parent or older visitor). Children can display models and paintings, or make up quizzes and games, use word-processing for impressive collaborative writing or use a simple database to record answers to their questionnaires. Assessment at Key Stage 1 will need to be through talking to and observing children engaged in these activities at intervals over the whole project because oral responses will be more detailed, more reflective and reveal more of their thinking strategies than is possible in writing, although labelled drawings and picture stories or stories with 'bubbles' could also be helpful.

Using planning suggestions in Figure 4.4 as a starting point, one Year 6 class in a suburban school investigated changes in population and settlement in their area; this was greatly influenced by the effects of the railway on a rural community. They began, using maps, census returns and street directories in the local library, to find out when their own houses had been built, who had lived in them and where they had moved from. Then they worked in groups to find out about the three buildings which had been the focus of the previous village community; the church, the farm and the manor house. An initially recalcitrant group researching the church had, by the end of term, constructed a large pottery model of it, complete with an electronic display board explaining features of historical interest which lit up when the relevant button was pressed. Audio tape dramatisation of related events and music and church lights seen through the stained glass created an impressive *son et lumière!* Another group investigated the timber-frame farm buildings which have now become the local DIY shop. The third group, peering over the gate of an apparently mock-Tudor detached house not dissimilar to the others in the road, was invited in to discover that it was an Elizabethan manor house, the prototype of the surrounding 1920s housing. This offered excellent opportunities to consider reasons for similarities and differences. Findings were presented in a slide show to friends and neighbours over afternoon tea.

In another school, a local study of a Year 3 class focused on a short period of time, the impact of World War II on the local community, after noticing alterations to a house which a local paper confirmed was bomb damage. After a video-recorded interview with the elderly inhabitants and using a variety of sources, the children worked in groups to attempt to reconstruct life in the house over the decades before, during and after the war. These reconstructions were presented through drama and the popular dances and songs of each decade. The 1950s reconstruction included a Coronation party in which the event was described by talking heads using contemporary newspaper accounts from inside a cardboard box 'television'.

	Starting point (evidence)	Activity
Family	Photographs	Collect photographs of self/family. Put them in sequence/on a time-line. Describe changes, similarities and differences.
	Artefacts	Collect 'old things'. Make a museum. Try to place exhibits in sequence. Explain what they tell us about the past.
	Visit site, museum, gallery:	Site: role-play, models, plans, drawings, stories.
	Site whst happended here . . . ?	
	Museum what is it for? How is it made/used?	Museum: drawings, explanations, use/examine artefacts.
	Gallery clothes, furniture or narrative, in paintings.	Gallery: role-play, stories about pictures (wear clothes – e.g. Geffrye Museum). Sort and name materials in clothes.
	Oral	Questionnaires, interviews, film and video
Locality	Buildings (houses, shops, church, farm, offices, civic buildings)	Observe changes in structure, materials, purpose: draw, model, photograph.
	Photographs, paintings, old postcards	Look for what they tell us about the past, similarities and differences.
	Maps	Look for differences, explain.
	Oral	Interviews, questionnaires, stories.
	Written sources - old birthday cards, gravestones, birth certificates, family leners	What do they tell us?
Story	Family stories	Oral Read, discuss, retell, rewrite, draw, act.
	Local stories	Books
	Stories about events in the past	Picture-stories
	Famous people	Tapes
	Eye-witness accounts	Film
	Fiction	Video
	Myth and legend	Ballads & folk songs
		Plays
		Newspapers

Figure 4.3 Key Stage 1

Sources	Starting points	Activities
Maps Photos Pictures Newspapers Parish Records Census returns Gravestones Street directions Local histories Oral accounts Buildings Artefacts	An important historical issue, linked to national trends involving either: (a) an aspect of local history e.g. education leisure – (holiday resort) religion hospitals a local industry (b) an aspect of local history over a short period of time (c) an aspect of local history illustrating developments taught in another unit.	(a) Groups could research different buildings within the theme (e.g. either schools, churches, places connected with leisure), correlating findings on time-lines, through discussion, make display. (b) Time selected may be chosen for particulary rapid change (e.g. introduction of railway) or because of a particular event (e.g. outbreak of war) or a particular personality. (c) Choice of unit illustrated would depend on resources in the locality e.g. a Roman fort or villa, Victorian building, Elizabethan house, or museum or gallery with a relevant collection (a railway, agricultrual, canal, maritime museum).
Cross-referenced to analyse use of different sources, incompleteness, bias, conformatory and non-conformatory evidence.		

Figure 4.4 Key Stage 2 – a local study

In a third local history study, Brigid Bolton, a Lancaster University student working with Year 6 children, used knowledge they had gained through a study of Victorian Britain (the effects of steam power on the growth of railways, and mining and mass production in northern cities) as a basis for a local study focusing on Victorian Ambleside and the growth of tourism.

'Me' Years 1 and 2 – Key Stage 1 levels 1–3

This topic mainly reflects the first of the three areas of study of the Key Stage 1 history programme, changes in the everyday lives of the children and in the lives of familiar adults. The fourth focus, 'Stories', could be extended to include the other two areas, stories about famous men and women and famous events; this would allow opportunities to discuss why people did things and why events happened, the second of the key elements of enquiry. However, it is not necessary to include all aspects of the programme of study in one topic. A topic in the following year might focus on a period in the distant past, and involve stories about people and events through a theme such as 'castles'.

Years 1 and 2 worked on the theme 'Me' with a history focus. Year 1 concentrated on their own time-lines for six years, which recorded their own experiences of change over time. They brought in their own baby clothes, and toys they had had over the previous five years, sequenced socks and mittens to illustrate growth, sequenced their photographs, and recounted memories. They interviewed one of the parents about a new baby who was brought into school, weighed, measured and compared with them. They listed their achievements since they were babies: talking, throwing and catching balls, and so on. The children were also paired with Year 6 children as part of the Year 6 work on 'human development'. Each pair worked on a cross-curricular theme planned by the older child for a week, at their own level. One pair, for instance, studied an old oil lamp, wrote about it, painted it and found out about it, each in their own way, then they put the resulting work in a book and discussed similarities and differences of the five-year-old and ten-year-old approaches. Both the Year 1 and Year 6 children enjoyed this, and it enabled the younger children to predict what they may be like and able to do when they are 'twice as old as now'.

The Year 1 teacher and the head teacher also participated 'at their own level'. The Year 1 teacher made her own time-line illustrated with photographs of her family and key events in her life, concluding with her Graduation Day and her wedding. Since she was twenty-five, this was a very long time-line, and allowed the children to discuss their life span in relation to hers, and to compare different scales for recording time. The teacher displayed her own collection of books and toys, surrounding her wedding dress on a stand in the middle of the room and

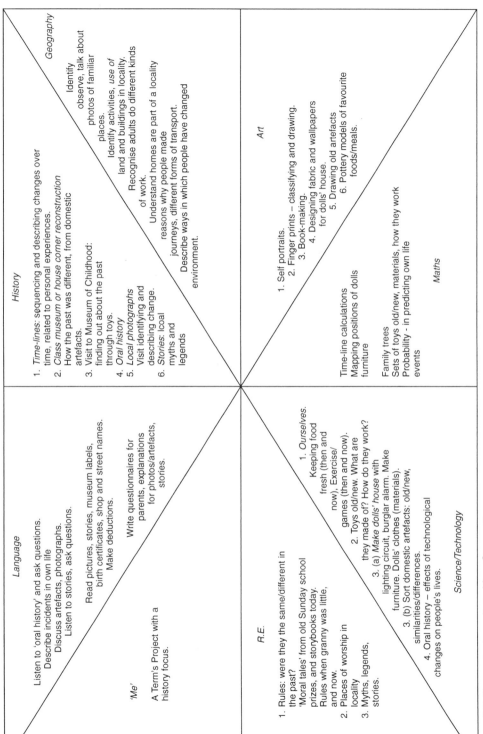

Figure 4.5 Core study unit 1. Key Stage 1

History

1. *Time-lines:* sequencing and describing changes over time, related to personal experiences.
2. *Class museum or house corner reconstruction* How the past was different, from domestic artefacts.
3. Visit to Museum of Childhood: finding out about the past through toys.
4. *Oral history*
5. *Local photographs* Visit identifying and describing change.
6. *Stories:* local myths and legends

Geography

Identify observe, talk about photos of familiar places.
Identify activities, *use of* land and buildings in locality.
Recognise adults do different kinds of work.
Understand homes are part of a locality reasons why people made journeys, different forms of transport.
Describe ways in which people have changed environment.

Art

1. Self portraits.
2. Finger prints – classifying and drawing.
3. Book-making.
4. Designing fabric and wallpapers for dolls' house.
5. Drawing old artefacts
6. Pottery models of favourite foods/meals.

Maths

Time-line calculations
Mapping positions of dolls furniture

Family trees
Sets of toys old/new, materials, how they work
Probability - in predicting own life events

Language

Listen to 'oral history' and ask questions.
Describe incidents in own life
Discuss artefacts, photographs.
Listen to stories, ask questions.

Read pictures, stories, museum labels, birth certificates, shop and street names.
Make deductions.

Write questionnaires for parents, explanations for photos/artefacts, stories.

'Me'

A Term's Project with a history focus.

R.E.

1. Rules: were they the same/different in the past?
'Moral tales' from old Sunday school prizes, and storybooks today. Rules when granny was little, and now.
2. Places of worship in locality
3. Myths, legends, stories.

Science/Technology

1. *Ourselves.* Keeping food fresh (then and now), Exercise/ games (then and now).
2. Toys old/new. What are they made of? How do they work?
3. (a) *Make dolls' house* with lighting circuit, burglar alarm. Make furniture. Dolls' clothes (materials)
3. (b) Sort domestic artefacts: old/new, similarities/differences.
4. Oral history – effects of technological changes on people's lives.

What I want children to learn	What I want children to do	Assessment opportunities
To communicate awareness and understanding of history in the following ways: (i) sequencing objects and events in order to develop a sense of chronology	Time-lines Make own time-line 0–7 (i) place photographs of themselves in sequence on time-line (ii) compare with time-line for teacher; use words such as then, now	*Level 1* Can sequence photographs, events. Can recognise the distinction between past and present in their lives; in teacher's life: can use language such as now, then, next, before, after. Can use questionnaire to answer questions about their own lives
(ii) using words and phrases relating to the passing of time (iii) finding out about aspects of the past through learning to ask and answer questions which help to identify (a) differences between past and present (b) different ways in which the past is represented using artefacts	(i) bring in 'old things' for house corner role-play/class museum Draw them; attach (by Velcro, which allows rearrangement) to a sequence line with categories (very old/old/new). (ii) Visit Museum of Childhood. Handling session - old toys What were they made of? What are they? How did they work?	*Level 1* Beginning to find out about the past from sources of information and to recognise a distinction between past and present *Level 2* Also beginning to identify some of the different ways in which the past is represented, and to answer questions about the past from sources of information through making books or presentation for grandparents, or tape or video recordings for 'Children's TV or radio' can:
Oral sources	(i) write questionnaire for granny, grandad, or older person about life when they were little, or tape-record interview at home	*Level 1* recognise distinction between past and present, in other people's lives

Figure 4.6 'Me' history grid

	(ii) invite several older people who were brought up in different parts of the world and in different circumstances to tell children about their early years, to show photographs of themselves in the past and of their treasured possessions.	*Level 2* identify some of the different ways in which the past is represented *Level 1* ask and answer questions about photographs which recognise similarities and differences using concepts of time
Photographs	Collect and display selected old photographs of locality; take photographs of/visit same sites today	*Level 2* also demonstrate factual knowledge about events or people beyond living memory, related to photographs
Stories	(i) invite someone from a local history society to tell 'true stories' about locality which children can retell, draw, act out	*Level 1* can sequence events and use time vocabulary in retelling stories
	(ii) myths and legends from different cultures	*Level 2* also can begin to explain why people acted as they did, demonstrate factual knowledge learned from 'true stories' and ask and answer questions about the past, based on the stories

Figure 4.6 cont

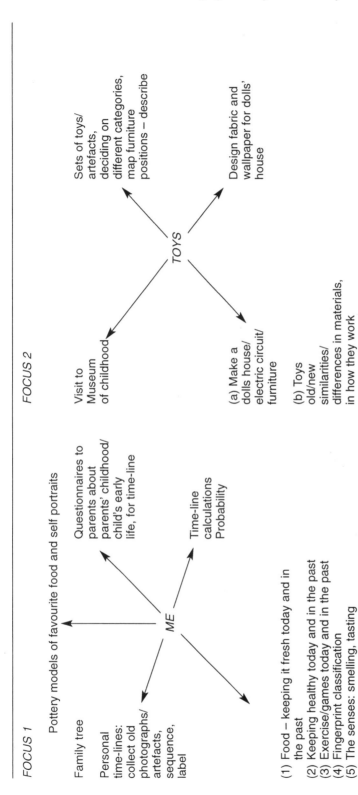

Figure 4.7 Plan showing how work for the term was organised around four Focuses, each several weeks

FOCUS 1

Pottery models of favourite food and self portraits

Family tree

Personal
time-lines:
collect old
photographs/
artefacts,
sequence,
label

ME

(1) Food – keeping it fresh today and in
    the past
(2) Keeping healthy today and in the past
(3) Exercise/games today and in the past
(4) Fingerprint classification
(5) The senses: smelling, tasting

Questionnaires to
parents about
parents' childhood/
child's early
life, for time-line

Time-line
calculations
Probability

FOCUS 2

Visit to
Museum
of childhood

TOYS

Sets of toys/
artefacts,
deciding on
different categories,
map furniture
positions – describe

Design fabric and
wallpaper for dolls'
house

(a) Make a
dolls house/
electric circuit/
furniture

(b) Toys
old/new
similarities/
differences in materials,
in how they work

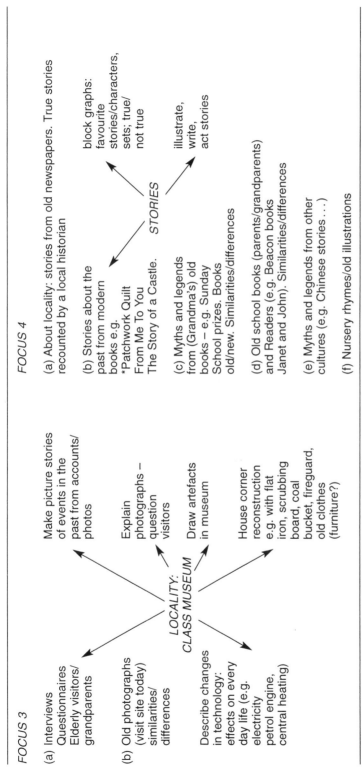

FOCUS 3

(a) Interviews
Questionnaires
Elderly visitors/
grandparents

Make picture stories
of events in the
past from accounts/
photos

(b) Old photographs
(visit site today)
similarities/
differences

Explain
photographs –
question
visitors

Draw artefacts
in museum

*LOCALITY:
CLASS MUSEUM*

Describe changes
in technology:
effects on every
day life (e.g.
electricity
petrol engine,
central heating)

House corner
reconstruction
e.g. with flat
iron, scrubbing
board, coal
bucket, fireguard,
old clothes
(furniture?)

FOCUS 4

(a) About locality: stories from old newspapers. True stories
recounted by a local historian

(b) Stories about the
past from modern
books e.g.
*Patchwork Quilt
From Me To You
The Story of a Castle.*

block graphs:
favourite
stories/characters,
sets; true/
not true

STORIES

(c) Myths and legends
from (Grandma's) old
books – e.g. Sunday
School prizes. Books
old/new. Similarities/differences

illustrate,
write,
act stories

(d) Old school books (parents/grandparents)
and Readers (e.g. Beacon books
Janet and John). Similarities/differences

(e) Myths and legends from other
cultures (e.g. Chinese stories. . . .)

(f) Nursery rhymes/old illustrations

Note: * V. Flournoy (1987) *The Patchwork Quilt.* Puffin.
P. Rogers (1987) *From Me To You.* Orchard Books.
J. S. Goodall (1986) *The Story of a Castle.* Andre Deutsch.

Figure 4.7 cont

invited her own grandma to come to school! Gran, teacher, and children, all enjoyed exchanging memories. Meanwhile, in the foyer, the head teacher, who was new to the school, took the opportunity both to introduce herself and to support the history project, by making her time-line. This was very long indeed because she was nearly 50 years old. She was able to show us photographs of her father leaving home to go to war and other very personal records – a long swathe of her golden hair, cut when she was five, her 50-year-old teddy, her first mitten. She told us in one assembly, a moving story of how she had found these things hidden in a secret box in her parents' home on their death. In other assemblies, she read to us moral tales from her parents' Sunday school prizes. This infant project developed excellent interpersonal understandings and insights throughout the whole-school community, at far more than eight levels!

The Year 2 extension of the theme was originally going to be 'when granny was little', but since grannies ranged in age from mid-thirties to about sixty, this was not a very useful title, and certainly did not go back to pre-electricity and horse-drawn carts. So they stuck to an extended version of 'me'. This was not a multicultural school, but a Chinese boy had recently joined the class. He spoke little English and did not adjust easily. The class teacher seized this opportunity to develop his work on 'when Mummy was little' into a rich subtheme on what it was like to grow up in Shanghai, with the help of the boy's mother. The class went to the Chinese exhibition, and went to see the Chinese New Year festivities in Soho. This led to work on old Chinese tales, with big collages and models of dragons and of the 'Willow Pattern Plate', work on Chinese paintings, experiments in writing with a Chinese brush in ink, and Chinese calendars and counting systems. The term concluded with a Chinese meal which Mrs Chan showed the children how to prepare, then they compared old China with what Mrs Chan told them about life in China today, and how life in Shanghai is different from and similar to life in Croydon! The Chinese work gave the project a far richer dimension and also led to greater personal understandings for all those involved.

Children's work

Some children's questionnaires for their parents ask about the arrival of cats, dogs, goldfish, brothers and sisters, about holidays, cuts and bruises, or moving home. This six-year-old however, is already preoccupied with self-assessment and monitoring her progress!

The information from the questionnaire was transferred to the time-line There were great opportunities here for transactional writing and for parental involvement. Parental understanding and support is particularly important in family history which can be a sensitive area. The family tree was optional and done with help at home.

1 When did I first have our first tooth?
 I had my first tooth at five months old
2 When did I first Walk?
 I first walked at 9 Months.
3 When did I first dress our selvs?
 I first dressed at 18 Months
4 When did I First Read a book?
 When I Was 4 years old
5 When did I First draw?
 When I Was 2 years old
6 When did I Start to write?
 I Started to write When I Was 4 years
7 When did I have Money?
 When I Was 3 years old
8 When did I Know my numbers?
 I knew my numbers When I was 4 years

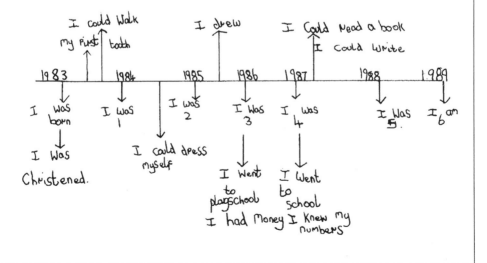

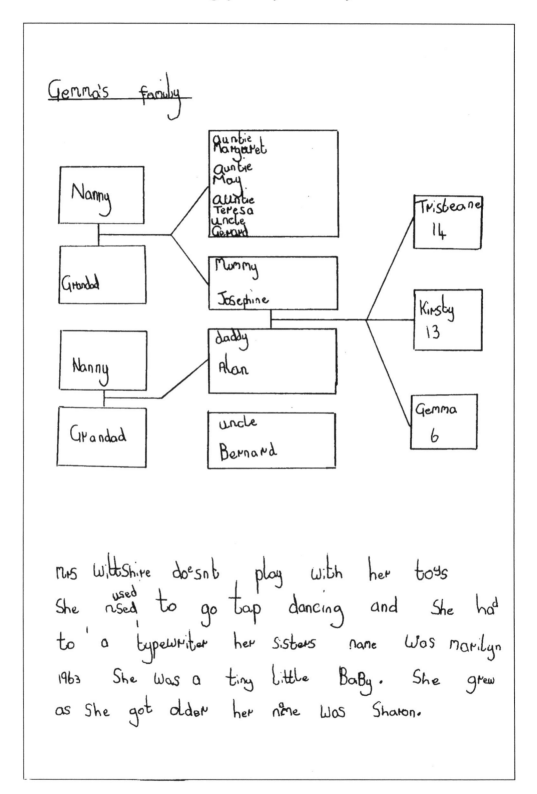

Gemma's family

Nanny

Grandad

Nanny

Grandad

Auntie Margaret
Auntie May
auntie Teresa
uncle Gerard

Mummy
Josephine

daddy
Alan

uncle
Bernard

Trisbeane 14

Kirsty 13

Gemma 6

Mrs Wiltshire doesnt play with her toys
She used to go tap dancing and She had
to ' a typewriter her sisters name was marilyn
1963 She was a tiny little Baby. She grew
as She got older her name was Sharon.

OUR TRIP TO BETHNAL GREEN
TOY MUSEUM.

On Wednesday, 14th June, we went on the
coach to the toy museum.
The coach driver took us to the wrong
museum. We had to go on the underground
When we got to the toy museum James had
a nosebleed.
In the museum we saw old toys:
Trains, cars, dolls, games, soldiers,
puppets, doll's houses, boats, teddy bears,
horses and theatres.
We found out that old toys were made from
wood and our new toys are made from plastic.
WE found out that dolls were made out of
wood, wax, china, clay, paper and plastic
lots of old dolls had real hair.
We had a talk about old toys—it was very
interesting.
We were tired when we got home.

A Story by Class 7.

Gemma

Toys

My grandprents would
have played With
hoops and ropes

dolls

Doll were made out of clay and wax wood and paper and china and we saw tooth brush dolls and we saw a plug face and we saw Queen Victoria and the dolls hair was real and our dolls don t have real hair and we saw toy town

The children were very interested to use the information in their time-lines, photographs and collections of toys to make deductions about the past, and about changes over time. These were certainly 'interactive' displays.

The account of the visit to the Museum of Childhood is a piece of shared writing. It refers, in a very sanguine way, to the initial excitement of the day, when the coach driver deposited the children outside Burlington Arcade, telling the teacher, 'It's just up the road love' (assuming they were going to the Museum of Mankind!). Although she had made a preliminary visit, the teacher assumed that this was another entrance. The novelty of the tube journey from Piccadilly Circus to Bethnal Green was so exciting that James had a nosebleed before they were able to discuss such concepts as continuity and change, similarity and difference, during the 'handling session' led by the museum staff. Later, they wrote a book explaining how the toys in the past were sometimes different from theirs, and why.

Ancient Greece Years 5 and 6 – Key Stage 2 Core Study Unit 4

Years 5 and 6 worked together on this project, in a shared 'open plan' area. It began with children deciding to set up a travel agency in a corner of the room, in order to find out what Greece is like today. Eleven-year-olds – boys and girls – often enjoy the excuse for this sort of role-play. They collected brochures, timetables and posters from local travel agents, made and displayed their own information sheets, booklets and booking forms, and enclosed the corner behind net curtains suspended from the ceiling. They set up a reception area with easy chairs, installed a computer, telephones (unconnected) and coffee-making facilities! Their efficiency compared favourably with the shop in the High Street. Having planned their holidays, everyone made themselves an effective passport (photocopying the front of a passport on to yellow paper and sticking this on to black card, with their school photograph inside) and filled in a booking form. The booking form involved complex calculations of time, speed and distance, money, and also of weight; a collection of possible luggage items was made in a suitcase, ranging from snorkels and sun cream to 'evening wear', which was weighed so that suitable choices within the luggage allowance could be made. Later in the term, one group used the information they had acquired to make a video tape of a 'Travel Programme' about Greece. Groups also took it in turns to cook a Greek lunch once a week, with the help of a parent, and invited a chosen guest. (It was a school tradition to cook a meal on the theme of the class project.)

The travel agency led into the second focus, finding out about changes within Ancient Greek civilisation, by making a time-line, supported by maps, showing key events, people and architecture. The study unit (giving an overview of the period) was introduced through class lessons, describing and explaining the broad historical canvas. This was a useful exercise in note-taking. The notes were then used to make individual time-lines.

The children learned a great deal of mathematics in making their models of Greek temples. This involved choosing a photograph of a particular temple, finding out or estimating its dimensions, reducing these to one-hundredth the actual size, then drawing the nets to make the model: a series of cuboids for the steps, cylinders for the pillars, a triangular prism for the roof or portico. They then had to describe their model using listed concepts: angles, edges, faces, height, length, area. This is a useful mathematics assessment exercise because the models varied in complexity, and so did the descriptions, from 'my model has twenty-four right angles' to 'the area of the right-angle triangles forming the end faces of the triangle-based prism is 50 sq. cm'. Number patterns attributed to Pythagoras were a useful entry into triangle and square numbers and Pythagoras' theorem. Learning about and using the Greek counting system was also a good way of testing children's understanding of place value. One child told us that this reminded him of the 'golden rectangle'. Since the teacher was not knowledgeable on this subject, he brought in his book and explained it to everyone!

The Golden Rectangle.

The construction of a Golden Rectangle begins with a square (shaded). Which is divided into two parts, by the line E to F. This (Point F) is the centre of a circle whose radius is the diagonal line F to C. An arc of the circle is drawn (C to G) and the base line (A to D) is extended to join with it. This becomes the base of the rectangle. The new side (H to G) is now drawn at right angles to the new base, and the line is brought out to meet it. The ratio between the sides in a golden rectangle is 1 : 1·6. The golden rectangle is a satisfying shape for a building.

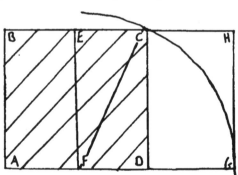

The third focus was on myths and legends. This was related to music-making in Ancient Greece, a convenient way of integrating the science attainment target on sound, which the whole school had decided to tackle. The British Museum leaflet on Greek musical instruments was an excellent introduction to Ancient Greek stringed and wind instruments, which, we learned, might accompany recited poetry. First, children experimented to discover the variables influencing

<u>Science investigation. - Sound.</u>

<u>What we wanted to find out.</u>

We wanted to find out how we could change the note of a string.

<u>What we did.</u>

First we put an elastic band round a cup a plucked it, to make a sound. First we changed the thickness of the band. The thicker band made a lower sound. Then we changed the tightness of the band. The Tighter band made a higher sound. Then we Put a pencil under the ×cub× cup. The pencil changed the sound to a lower sound.

<u>Conclusion.</u>

We found out that you could change the note of a band by a) Thickening the band b) Change the tightness of the band c) putting ·on·· a pencil under the cup.

How we made a string Instrument.

Task.

      What we had to do was to make a string Instrument with notes tuned to a musical scale. [!]
of different pitch.

What we did.

First we got a piece of wood and we banged 3 nails in. (A,B and C.) Then we got 'string J' and tied one end to 'nail A'. We then banged in nails D and G and wound string J round nail D and fastened it to nail G. We then did the same with the other 2 strings (K and L) and it finished off like this:

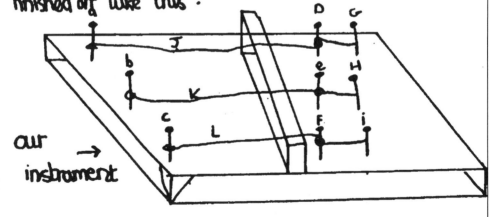

our → instrument

The Whirlpool.

Verse 1.

Between two rocks, near Syran island.
lies the whirlpool.
Water twisting.
Swirling, whirling, foam unfurling.
Sucking ships into its vortex.

Verse 2.

Six headed Scylla hungrily waits,
In her cave,
Suddenly moving;
Swirling, whirling, foam unfurling.
Swallowing men on passing ships.

Verse 3.

Ulysses ship sailed near the rocks,
survived the whirlpool,
faced the monster.
Swirling, whirling, foam unfurling,
Scylla ate 6 men - then safety.

pitch, then they each designed and constructed an instrument on which a series of four notes of different pitch could be played. This produced an ingenious variety of solutions. They then wrote poems based on stories in the *Odyssey* to be accompanied on their instrument! One group decided to make a tape-recording of a programme for schools explaining how they had done this, before recording their poem.

Another addition to the theme was the news that Derek Walcott, the West Indian poet, had been awarded the W. H. Smith Literary Award for his poem *Omeros*, which transposes the Homer stories of Hector, Achilles and the fought-over Helen to a fishing community in St Lucia. It also includes a dream-like fantasy of a West Indian wandering in exile in Europe and the story of Philoctetes, a yam-keeper with a 'symbolic wound' inherited from the 'chained ankles of his grandfather'. It cannot be pretended that we read all 325 pages, but the story did offer an unexpected multicultural dimension to Homer, as Walcott puts it, transported, 'across centuries of the sea's parchment atlas'. A PGCE student working in a multicultural school, subsequently achieved some wonderful poetry from Year 6 children with Greek, Turkish and Caribbean backgrounds, after reading them Leon Garfield's version of the Prometheus story in *The God Beneath the Sea*.

The fourth focus was based on a visit to the British Museum. Each group of three or four children chose a particular showcase in Room 69 to study, drawing artefacts and taking notes from labels, in order to find out about different aspects of life in Ancient Greece. In school, they then designed and made an impressive museum, raised on staging blocks, with a facade from floor to ceiling consisting of pillars made from rolls of corrugated card painted grey, supporting a pediment decorated by enlarging photocopies of motifs from a Greek frieze. The exhibits, labelled and explained in the brochure, were mainly drawings of artefacts seen in the British Museum, replica pottery, some modern Greek holiday souvenirs, and large posters made by projecting slides of pictures on Greek vases and copying the image accurately. These were used as evidence exercises, as in 'The Hoplite Race' quoted in the examples of work (p.79).

An interesting opportunity occurred for the children to extend the teachers' plans in an unexpectedly successful way, towards the end of term. They had been watching a television programme about archaeology in Greece. Prompted by this, one group asked if they could see what they could find in the rough area of school grounds. Not expecting them to find anything of interest, the teacher suggested they mark off a square metre, and dig for twenty minutes. The results, in an area which had previously been allotments, proved so exciting that a number of other groups ended up undertaking a systematic excavation, which revealed broken pottery, a variety of old bottles (from Victorian to HP Sauce), clay pipes, parts of tools, plumbing, and old shoes. When they unearthed a tractor tyre and the beginning of some steps, they decided 'there may have been a farm house here'. Someone decided to go to the local library for further information; someone else sought out people who had lived in the area for some time, to question them. The children spontaneously decided to make a scale plan of the 'site' where the artefacts had been found. These were carefully measured and drawn, and put on a time-line in estimated sequence, in order to guess what they might tell us about the site before the school was built. The children did most of this in their spare time, no tetanus jabs were required, and it proved an excellent way of evaluating the historical thinking processes they had learned and were able to transfer.

Finally, it seems important to stress that neither of the teachers had any specialist knowledge of Ancient Greece, and since the project took place in the Spring term after a very short Christmas break, they had little preparation time. Their own initial reading was limited to a selection of children's books from the local library, and to *The Times Atlas of Ancient Civilizations* (1989). It is salutary that teachers do not need to feel inadequate if they do not have specialist knowledge of a period as long as they are prepared to share the excitement of the learning process. This is probably of greater educational value. (However, we were told that 'The Golden Age of Greece' is a Victorian idea, no longer held by historians!)

Children's work

Filling in the holiday booking form designed by the travel agency involved collaborative calculations: reading timetables, the 24-hour clock, understanding time zones, ratio and distances, reading calendars, weight and money calculations involving large numbers, approximation, and the four rules of number.

Large, carefully observed white-on-black paintings taken from projected slides of pictures on Greek vases decorated the class museum and were a basis for discussion of what they might tell us about Ancient Greece.

The British Museum booklet on the role of women in Ancient Greece, which contained quotations from contemporary male and female writers, seemed a good subject for discussion. This child's writing, however, shows how difficult it is to make a distinction between attitudes and values today and in the past, and the reasons why they may be different. Maybe the issue was too complex or the discussion not sufficiently structured by the teacher. Nevertheless, there is an incipient understanding that life in Ancient Greece was different. The child has applied her knowledge from another source that women had no political voice, then used this as a yardstick against society today, both in Britain and in other places. Although the ideas seem incoherent, there is evidence of reasoning, of recognising that the past was different, and yet some issues remain similar.

Maths
(a) *Set up travel agency*
   (i) Plan, book and cost holiday
   (ii) Luggage allowance
   (iii) Route. Journey times
(b) *Make model of chosen*
   Greek temple (nets, scale, properties of cylinders cuboids, prisms)
(c) Pythagoras △ □ numbers numbers theorem golden rectangle
(d) *Olympic Games* (BM notes). Measuring speed, distance, variables affecting projectiles.
(e) Time-line (scale, measure).

History
(a) *Time-line 1600BC–0* Class lessons, secondary sources to mark 4 periods and key events, people
(b) *The Fall of Troy* Read about excavations and stories from the *Odyssey*
(c) *Visit British Museum* Find out in groups about variety of aspects of Greek life. Draw artefacts and note information Set up class museum and/or make travel brochure explaining what artefacts tell us about Ancient Greece. Interpretations. Pictures from later periods portraying children in Ancient Greece.
(d) *Interpretations.* Pictures from later periods portraying children in Ancient Greece.

English
(a) Stories from *Odyssey*, legends, myths, contemporary accounts.
(b) Debate the role of women in Ancient Greece.
(c) Explanations: science experiments; deductions from evidence.
(d) Travel programme video.
(e) Notes and reference work.
(f) Museum brochure.
(g) Travel agents literature.
(h) Stories – explain constellations then and now.
(i) Poetry writing.

Geography
Set up travel agency.
Make travel programme.
Find out where Greece is and what it is like: maps – towns, relief: climate.
How do people live – food
How do you get there?
How long does it take?

Maps of Europe, Greece, Mediterranean, Asia, in ancient times.

Science/Technology
(a) Sound Pythagoras
   (i) Find out about Greek musical instruments (IBM teachers' notes)
   (ii) Experiments to discover variables influencing pitch (length, thickness, tautness)
   (iii) Design and make your own instrument which plays 4 notes in sequence
   (iv) Pythagoras' discovery of relationship between length, vibration and pitch.
(b) Volume experiments (Archimedes).
(c) Space. Constellations – (Greek myths). Plot positions of stars on grids.

Music
(a) Write 'music' to accompany your *Odyssey* poem, using own musical symbols.
(b) Play it.
(c) Make tape explaining how to do this for other groups of children.

Art
(a) Drawings from Greek vases (for evidence exercise and museum).
(b) Screen printing – Greek motifs.
(c) Postcards (from 'Greek' holiday).
(d) Posters for Travel Agent.
(e) Wall painting. The Trojan Horse (true or false?).
(f) Greek Museum (+ design and technology).

R.E.
Myths
What questions did people in Ancient Greece ask, and how did they answer them?

Figure 4.8 Core study unit 4. Key Stage 2 – Ancient Greece

What I want children to learn	What I want children to do	Assessment opportunities
•To place within a chronological framework: events, people and changes in the history of Ancient Greece 1600BC – 0BC To use dates and terms relating to the passing of time, including ancient, modern, BC, AD, century, decade and terms which define different periods	(i) Make time-line 1600BC–0 Mark four periods, key events, people, architecture 1600–1150BC Mycenean 1000–479BC Expansion 478–405BC Golden Age 336–30BC Hellenistic (ii) Find out about each period. Write notes e.g. Mycenean metal work Mycenean beehive tombs Mycenean writings; fall of Mycenae	*Level 3* Can make sets of 'Ancient Greek' and 'not Ancient Greek'. Can describe to an audience changes indicated by the time-line, using some dates and special vocabulary. Can explain a key event, for example, why as one of Xerxes' soldiers you were defeated
•To learn about the characteristic features of each period from reference books containing photographs of artefacts, buildings, sites	Greek emigration to Asia Minor, Black Sea, Africa, trade city states, farming, Persian wars and victory of Athens Greek temples, Athenian democracy, theatres, Socrates, war between Athens and Sparta	*Level 4* Can describe different features of one of these periods (in groups) from information collected
•To describe changes explain reasons for and results of situations make links between main changes and events	Alexander the Great – Empire in N. Africa and Asia Greek medicine, mathematics and science Olympic Games, theatre (iii) draw maps to illustrate changes, marking significant places, dates, routes	*Level 5* Can identify 'military' events (fall of Mycaenae, defeat of Persia, defeat of Athens, Alexander's Empire) and say how they caused other changes described by time-line *Level 3* Can offer archaeological and legendary information about Troy

Figure 4.9 Ancient Greece history grid

•To identify and give reasons for different ways in which the past is represented and interpreted	(i) from secondary sources find out about archaeological excavations around possible sites of Troy (ii) read stories from the Trojan Wars (*Iliad*) and stories about the journey of Odysseus (*Odyssey*)	
	(iii) 'Dig' in waste area of school grounds Draw a diagram of site and measure in square metres Collect 'finds' Draw and record plan where found	*Level 4* Can write archeologist's reports saying what artefact found in the school 'dig' tells us for certain about the past, what reasonable guesses can be made about it and what cannot be known
		Level 5 The story of the Trojan Horse, true or false? Divide paper into two columns and list factual and legendary evidence
•To find out about Ancient Greece from: reference books artefacts in British Museum (Room 69) resources related to British Museum visit (slides, postcards, information sheets on musical instruments, textiles, lives of women, Olympic Games)	Visits to British Museum (Room 69)	*Level 3* Can write explanatory label for artefact drawn in British Museum (or for musical instrument, model temple or Greek vase painting) *Level 4* Can write a brochure for museum or for tourists to Greece, using variety of sources *Level 5* Can group sources used in brochure or presentation and explain usefulness in investigating a particular aspect of everyday life.
•To describe and explain to others orally and in writitng, individually and in	Display drawings (and postcards and clay models) in a 'class museum'	

Figure 4.9 cont

groups, the products of their investigations related to:

- time-lines
- models of Greek temples
- 'Greek' musical instruments to accompany stories from the *Odyssey*, tape-recorded
- brochures and posters made for the travel agency
- inferences made from Greek vase paintings which are explored in a variety of artistic media
- museum of Ancient Greece
- display and explanation of 'finds' in 'school dig'

Write labels explaining what they tell us about life in Ancient Greece

Take visitors on guided tour of 'museums' or other classroom displays and explain significance

To be able to discuss, as result of these investigations, the links between Ancient Greece and the modern world (e.g. in literature, language, mathematics, architecture, art, politics, sport).

Figure 4.9 cont

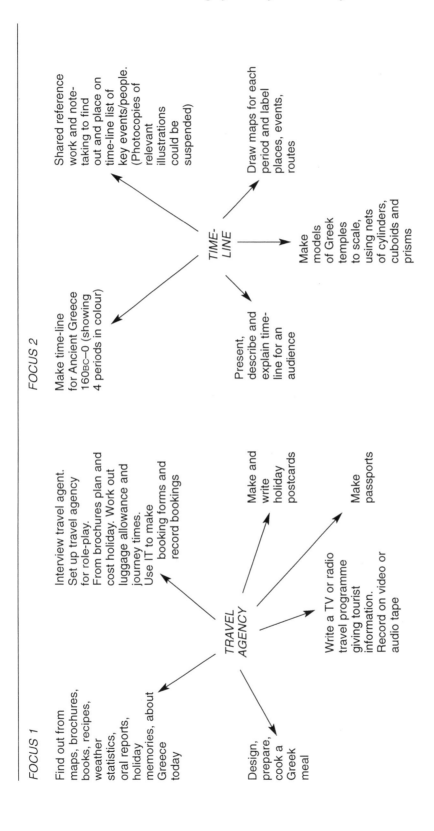

Figure 4.10 Plan showing how work for the term was organised around four focuses

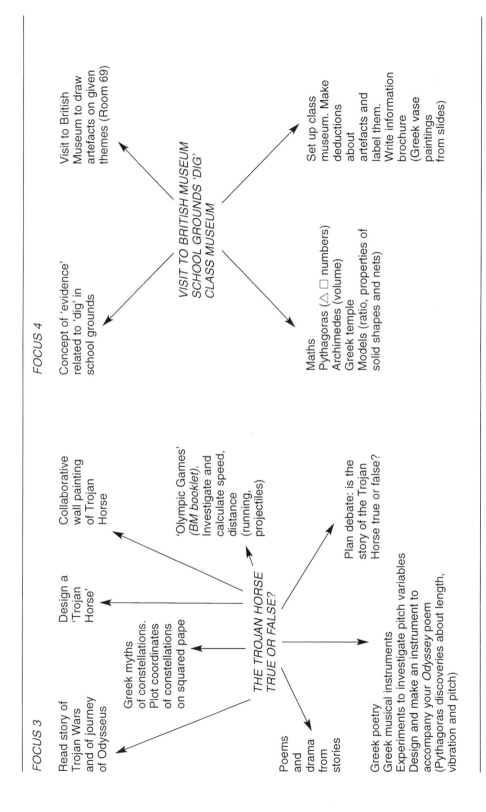

FOCUS 3

Read story of Trojan Wars and of journey of Odysseus

Design a 'Trojan Horse'

Collaborative wall painting of Trojan Horse

Greek myths of constellations. Plot coordinates of constellations on squared pape

'Olympic Games' (*BM booklet*). Investigate and calculate speed, distance (running, projectiles)

THE TROJAN HORSE TRUE OR FALSE?

Plan debate: is the story of the Trojan Horse true or false?

Poems and drama from stories

Greek poetry
Greek musical instruments
Experiments to investigate pitch variables
Design and make an instrument to accompany your *Odyssey* poem
(Pythagoras discoveries about length, vibration and pitch)

FOCUS 4

Concept of 'evidence' related to 'dig' in school grounds

VISIT TO BRITISH MUSEUM SCHOOL GROUNDS 'DIG' CLASS MUSEUM

Visit to British Museum to draw artefacts on given themes (Room 69)

Set up class museum. Make deductions about artefacts and label them. Write information brochure (Greek vase paintings from slides)

Maths
Pythagoras (△ ☐ numbers)
Archimedes (volume)
Greek temple
Models (ratio, properties of solid shapes and nets)

Figure 4.10 cont

BOOKING FORM

Travellers Katie Snowden, Susan Hailstones

Destination Cyprus Paphos

Accomodation The Annabelle four star hotel

Transport British airways 757

Distance 3600 km

Departure time 17.45

Arrival time 23.59

Duration of Journey 6hr.14mins - 2hr = 4hr.14mins

Speed 580 K.ph

Date of departure Monday 11th June

Luggage weight luggage allowance 20 Kgs

Cost per person £789 + £322 + £217 = £1248

Car Hire Metro £1550 x 14 = 217

Insurance £75

The huge mural of the Trojan Horse which the children painted dominated the 'book corner' and was a suitable background for reading Greek myths and legends. The children attempted to make a distinction between what was probably true and what was legend. This example shows that it is not difficult to suggest what is 'false' supported by a reason, because ..., or but ... True aspects are more difficult to define or justify, because both supporting evidence and the child's knowledge of it is very limited.

The Hoplite Race

On our wall we have a painting of a Greek vase. The picture on the vase shows 'The Hoplite Race,' one one of the races in the Greek Olympic games.

What We Know For Certain

They carried their shields ∴ they were very strong. They raced naked and did not wear any shoes. They wore their helmits and their shields were half as big as they were. Two shields are the same so they were on the same side. They were men.

What Reasnable Guesses Can We Make

It might have been at the beguining of the race because the runners are close together. It might be a race with just 4 people because there is 4 people on our picture. It might have been a relay because they might use there shields for batons. It might be a training sesion. Maybee they did not really wear their helmits and carry their shields. Maybee the bloke that did the painting put them in to show they were knights. Perhaps they carried their shields to test their strength.

What I would like to know.

I would like to know why did they not wear any clothes? Was it a relay? Why did they have their wepons? How tall and how old are the athletes? Were they married? Why was it painted in black and wright?

My thoughts

I disagree about. women are wretched and han to be their husbands slavo. Why cap'n t women go were ewerr they like with-out asb. asking thar husb'ands. Most women in the UK don't go to work but stay home to clean and look after children Most of the men in the UK oovn only see there children in the early morning and late evening.

Then again in anient Greece pealpe might think diffrently because the whole world was ditkert then. The anicent Greeks propaly had no say in the matter which is a big problem in todays parliament. There are still only a few women in parliament. But in ancient Greece women never voted. There are still place's in the world were this is true.

Surely, of all creatures that have life and will, we women
Are the most wretched. When for an extravagant sum,
We have bought a husband, we must then accept him as
Possessor of our body. This is to aggravate
Wrong with worse wrong. Then the great question:
  will the man
We get be bad or good? For women, divorce is not
Respectable; to repel the man, not possible

Euripides, Medea

Odyssey, True or False?

True	False
I think there was a prinsess that was captured but I am not so shure. shore (sure) that she was called Helen. I think there was a battle but I don't know think it hapened like the Odyssey says. I think there was a woman called Circe. I believe the syrans exsisted and sang thiler songs. I think that Ulysses wife was called penelope.	I do not think that there was a wooden horse because how could they have made it so big in a day. I do not believe a word of the Cyclops story for I do not believe in giants. I do not believe that Circe turned the men..it. into pigs but she might have cast a spell on them I do not think that scylla the six headed master exsisted but I do think there was a whirlpool.

Life in Tudor Times, study unit 2, Years 5 and 6

The unit on Life in Tudor Times began with an initial overview of the period; Henry VIII and the break with Rome, followed by rivalry with Spain over religion and trade in the 'New World' which led to the Armada of 1588. Key events were located on a class time-line. Two focuses were selected within this topic, one on 'Houses' and one on 'Ships'. These focuses were chosen because they allowed children to explore aspects of Tudor history which represent complex underlying changes, in ways which they could understand. 'Houses' included both a visit to Hampton Court, the showpiece of Henry VIII's new style of government and also to a nearby timber-frame Elizabethan house representing the increasing wealth of the new 'gentry'. 'Ships' began with a visit to the Mary Rose, which represented the beginnings of British sea power under Henry VIII, created as a defence after the break from Catholic Europe, and which led, in Elizabethan times, to exploration, an increase in trade and the emergence of a new class of merchants and 'gentry'. Rivalry with Spain in the 'New World' over trade resulted in the Armada of 1588, an event about which loyal British Roman Catholics felt ambivalent and which reflected conflicting loyalties and rivalries throughout Europe.

This unit allows children many opportunities to consider non-Eurocentric and non-Anglocentric perspectives. Firstly, the competition between Britain and Spain to find new routes to India and the East Indies, and the ensuing conflict in Central America and the West Indies allows children to use sources which reflect both cross-cultural influences and cultural conflict. A Schools Council booklet *Akbar and Elizabeth* (1983) shows teachers how they can help children to discover from Indian miniatures (in the Victoria and Albert Museum) the rich cultural influences of India on Elizabethan England by comparing clothes, buildings and garden design.

Often, sources which challenge Eurocentric perspectives can be selected from books for older children. In Roberts (1992: 22–5) there are excellent Mughal pictures of the rejoicing at the birth of Jahangir, son of Akbar the Great in 1569. The relief at the birth of an heir and also the idealistic representation of this event suggests similarities both between portraits of Elizabeth and her succession problems. It is interesting too that when Sir James Ross arrived at the Court of Jahangir, the Emperor thought most of the gifts from Europe were poor but he did like an English miniature portrait of a lady (a result of Indian influence on European art), and a map of India which he was given. However, Jahangir was not really interested in foreign rulers as he saw them as subordinates.

The Benin Empire was also at its peak at the same time as the Tudors were ruling England, which is when the British first arrived there. Sources about the

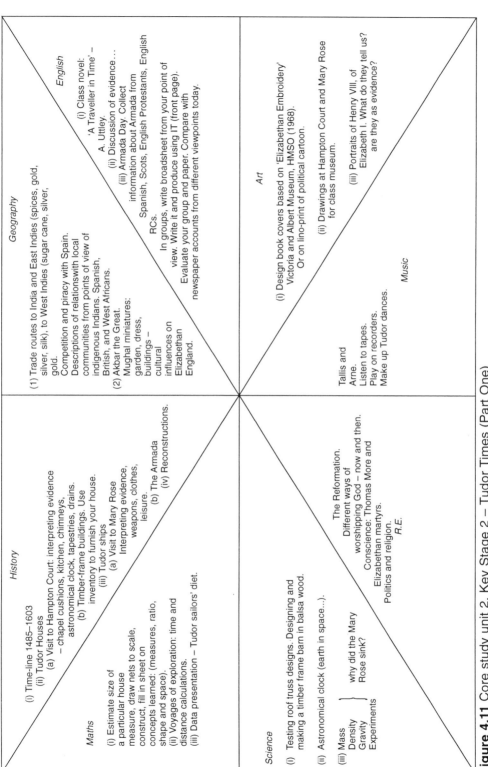

History

(i) Time-line 1485–1603
(ii) Tudor Houses
   (a) Visit to Hampton Court: interpreting evidence – chapel cushions, kitchen, chimneys, astronomical clock, tapestries, drains.
   (b) Timber-frame buildings. Use inventory to furnish your house.
(iii) Tudor ships
   (a) Visit to Mary Rose
      Interpreting evidence, weapons, clothes, leisure.
   (b) The Armada
      (iv) Reconstructions.

Geography

(1) Trade routes to India and East Indies (spices, gold, silver, silk), to West Indies (sugar cane, silver, gold.
Competition and piracy with Spain.
Descriptions of relations with local communities from points of view of indigenous Indians. Spanish, British, and West Africans.
(2) Akbar the Great.
Mughal miniatures: garden, dress, buildings – cultural influences on Elizabethan England.

English

(i) Class novel: 'A Traveller in Time' – A. Uttley.
(ii) Discussion of evidence....
(iii) Armada Day. Collect information about Armada from Spanish, Scots, English Protestants, English RCs.
In groups, write broadsheet from your point of view. Write it and produce using IT (front page).
Evaluate your group and paper. Compare with newspaper accounts from different viewpoints today.

Maths

(i) Estimate size of a particular house measure, draw nets to scale, construct, fill in sheet on concepts learned: (measures, ratio, shape and space).
(ii) Voyages of exploration: time and distance calculations.
(iii) Data presentation – Tudor sailors' diet.

Science

(i) Testing roof truss designs. Designing and making a timber frame barn in balsa wood.
(ii) Astronomical clock (earth in space...).
(iii) Mass
Density   } why did the Mary Rose sink?
Gravity
Experiments

R.E.

The Reformation.
Different ways of worshipping God – now and then.
Conscience: Thomas More and Elizabethan martyrs.
Politics and religion.

Art

(i) Design book covers based on 'Elizabethan Embroidery' Victoria and Albert Museum, HMSO (1968). Or on lino-print of political cartoon.
(ii) Drawings at Hampton Court and Mary Rose for class museum.
(iii) Portraits of Henry VIII, of Elizabeth I. What do they tell us? are they as evidence?

Music

Tallis and Arne.
Listen to tapes.
Play on recorders.
Make up Tudor dances.

Figure 4.11 Core study unit 2. Key Stage 2 – Tudor Times (Part One)

What I want children to learn: key elements	What I want children to do	Assessment opportunities:
• To place events, people, changes within a chronological framework • To use dates and terms relating to the passing of time (e.g. century, decade, Tudor, Elizabethan, court, monarch, civilisations, trade) To explain to others: Reasons for and results of events, situations, changes and to make links between events and situations	(i) Make a class time-line 1485–1603, put on key events learned through class lessons and reference work (e.g. related to Reformation, voyages of exploration, Armada, Monarchs)	*Level 3* Give a presentation to an audience, explaining the time-line with some explanation of causes and effect of events shown (e.g. of Reformation or of Drake's voyages to central America, or of Armada) *Level 4* Can use more factual information and more detailed explanations to play a 'chaining game' which involves (orally or through devising clue cards) thinking of all possible effects of an event
• To select, organise and communicate historical information • To identify characteristic features of the Tudor period: buildings, clothes, music, drama	(ii) In groups, use variety of resource materials to collect pictures and other information and make a book (or display) on one of the following, in Tudor times: homes of different kinds; work; leisure (including theatres and music); health; trade	*Level 5* Can devise a game involving selecting 'cause' or 'consequence' cards for a situation and explain what links there are between them (scoring based on number of reasonable causes/consequences identified) *Level 4* Can explain overarching and characteristic features of one of the group books
• Have some understanding of diversity of political and religious ideas, beliefs and attitudes of men and women in Tudor times • Describe and identify reasons for and results of Armada	Collect information about the Armada ('press releases' can be pre-selected by teacher) In groups (English Protestants, English Catholics, Dutch, Scottish, Spanish, French) write a broadsheet account from one of these perspectives	*Level 3* Can show a restricted perspective in broadsheet article *Level 4* Can try to explain a given perspective in a broadsheet article

Figure 4.12 Study unit 2: Life in Tudor Times

Objectives	Activities	Assessment
•Give reasons for different ways in which the past is represented and interpreted	Look at postcards of portraits from National Gallery of (a) Henry VIII (b) Elizabeth I	*Level 5* Can suggest reasons why events and personalities in broadsheets are portrayed differently
•Have some understanding of the reasons for the symbolism of and attitudes and values represented in portraits of Henry VIII and of Elizabeth I	(i) Discuss to what extent they tell what the person was really like, and what else (symbolism) they represent	*Level 3* Can explain why the portraits are idealised images
	(ii) Compare with written sources describing Henry VIII and Elizabeth I (given on p.??)	*Level 4* Can describe differences between written sources and portrait
		Level 5 Can explain why portraits and written sources tell different story
1. Ask questions and make deductions and inferences about life in Tudor Times from a variety of sources (a) at Hampton Court: e.g. tennis court (leisure) chapel (beliefs) furniture, kitchens, cellars (food, daily life) paintings, images of Henry VIII; the Field of the Cloth of Gold astronomical clock (understanding of time and space) (b) in Mary Rose Museum: e.g. the ship and its contents (clothes, tools, leisure, weapons, medicine)	1. Visit Hampton Court. Drawings and photographs used in school as clues to find out what they may tell us about Henry VIII and his court	*Level 3* Can make inferences from selected sources; and write explanatory label
		Level 4 Can combine inferences from several sources to write a poster, possibly using one piece of evidence to answer a question raised by another, e.g. how was the gun (on Mary Rose) fired?; use dates and special vocabulary where appropriate (e.g. court, monarch)
2. Organise findings, record and communicate to audience	2. Visit Mary Rose and Museum, Portsmouth. Use drawings and photographs as clues to find out about life on board a Tudor ship	*Level 5* Can select and evaluate sources using them in a structured way to make a book or a video investigating a historical question (e.g. who were the people on board the Mary Rose? Why did the Mary Rose sink?)
	Present information in poster or book or as a video or audio tape for an audience	

Figure 4.12 cont

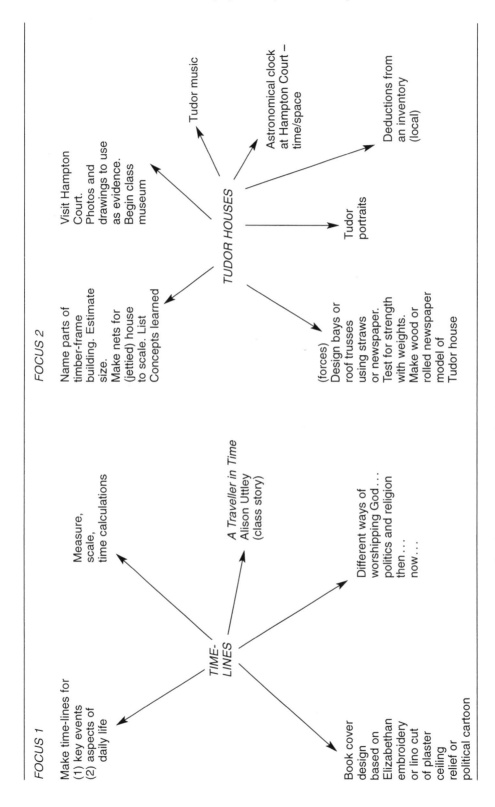

Figure 4.13 Plan showing how work for the term was organised around three Focuses

FOCUS 3

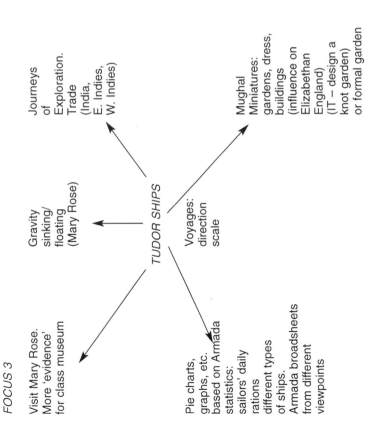

Visit Mary Rose.
More 'evidence'
for class museum

Gravity
sinking/
floating
(Mary Rose)

Journeys
of
Exploration.
Trade
(India,
E. Indies,
W. Indies)

TUDOR SHIPS

Voyages:
direction
scale

Pie charts,
graphs, etc.
based on Armada
statistics:
sailors' daily
rations
different types
of ships.
Armada broadsheets
from different
viewpoints

Mughal
Miniatures:
gardens, dress,
buildings
(influence on
Elizabethan
England)
(IT – design a
knot garden)
or formal garden

Figure 4.13 cont

Benin Kingdom can be found in the Museum of Mankind and the British Museum. They invite comparisons and contrasts with Tudor England; the mother of an Oba, or ruler, was of great importance, for example, and had her own palace and political power. Benin contained craft guilds of leather workers, weavers and blacksmiths. Written sources record its richly decorated palaces and houses. Extensive trade with Europe from the end of the fifteenth century included slaves. Smith (1992: 9) shows the crest of Sir John Hawkins, a successful English slave-trader of the sixteenth century, which he designed for himself and which depicts a defiant, captured African.

Similarly Green (1992) offers a picture of what life was like for the native peoples of the Americas, when Europeans first arrived and of how they perceived each other. For example, George Best who sailed with Martin Frobisher to North America wrote a detailed diary which is quoted, and there is also a contemporary painting of Frobisher's fight with an Inuit in 1577. From knowledge of such sources, children can develop a less Eurocentric and a more questioning attitude to life in Tudor times and view it from a range of perspectives.

As part of the focus on ships, both Year 5 and Year 6 spent two weeks finding out about the Armada. The competition between Britain and Spain to find new routes to India and the East Indies, and the ensuing conflict in central America and the West Indies, underlined by religious differences, was explained in class lessons. The viewpoints of different groups were discussed. How would the English Protestants feel, the English Catholics, the French, the Dutch, the Spanish? Why might the Scots be ambivalent? Children then worked in groups or individually to find out all they could about the daily progress of the Armada, making charts, maps and diaries. They made a display of daily rations for a Spanish and an English sailor, pie charts of the estimated food needed on a ship, and graphs showing ships of different kinds. Finally, each class worked in six groups together with the advisory teachers for ICT; by the end of a day, each group succeeded in producing a 'broadsheet' giving news of the Armada from the standpoint of a particular group. The French produced 'La Grenouille', the Spanish 'L'Escorial', the English Protestants 'The Golden Hind', the English Catholics 'The Priesthole', the Scots 'The Record' and the Dutch 'The Orange'.

Later, they evaluated the extent to which they had reflected different attitudes. These examples show that children are considering the reasons for behaviour and events.

The extracts from broadsheets representing different points of view were written on 'Armada Day'. They are based on 'press releases' and information in simulated teletext using 'Simtex', prepared by the Croydon Humanities adviser, Don Garman.

Models of Tudor timber-frame houses, based on particular examples, involved a range of mathematical concepts: measure, scale, properties of solid shapes.

LA GRENOUILLE

6f

10/7/1588

STAY OR DIE

The Duke of Madina Sidonia commented that if any Spanish Captain fails to maintain his position the penalty would be death, by hanging.
Soon the English are expected to run out of ammunition and surrender to the Spanish and the noble king Philip II is once more going to demonstrate his enormous power. We are all behind hm in the forthcoming final few battles at the sea.

THE PRIESTHOLE

1d

11th August 1588

SAIL AWAY, SAIL AWAY, SAIL AWAY

9 July 1588 6.0pm Captain Fleming of the Golden Hind has signalled the sighting of the Spanish fleet off the Lizard.
The tide will not allow the English fleet at Plymouth under Admiral Lord Howard of Effingham to put to sea till 9.0pm.
4 vessels of the English fleet managed to use their boats and anchors to warp out of Plymouth harbour before 9.0pm.
July 30 3.0pm Armada sighted by the English fleet to the south of Eddystone Lighthouse.
Beacons are reported to have been lit from Cornwall to London, local militia being organised to defend the English coastline.
July 31st the English pinnace Disdain opened fire off Plymouth at the rata encoranda.
At 9.0am this morning the Spanish flagship raised her national flag to signal the beginning.
After a four hour battle the Armada continues eastwood with the English in pursuit. Medina Sadonya gives the order for the fleet to form a cresent with the more heavily armed ships positioned at the horns. Drake reported to have left fleet during the night to investigate sails to the south.

The illustration on page 90 shows part of a child's self-evaluation sheet, made when he had finished his model, to explain the mathematics he thought he had learned in making it.

Britain and the wider world in Tudor times

The revised title of the study unit on life in Tudor times reflects recent scholarship which has done much to change perceptions of Elizabethan England. The study of the Armada from various perspectives could now include an Islamic perspective. For Matar (1999) has shown how the English were so afraid of 'popery' and of the Spanish that they became close allies with the

Mathematics
I learned Making
Tudor House Models.

length estimate measure	metres centimetre	I estimated the height of my house as 4·m.
Scale	1:100	The lenght of my house in real life would be 12m and on my model it is 12cm
Convert from one unit to another.	metres to cm cm to mm (to nearest mm)	The width of my house is 6m which on my model would be 6cm it could also be 6mm. 6m = 600cm = 6000mm
area rectangle triangle	cm² m²	the area of my first rectangle is 72cm². The area of my roof is 16cm²
volume of cuboid	cm³ m³	The volume of my 2nd cuboid is 252cm³.
Properties of solid shapes Cuboid	faces edges angles	On a cuboid there is 6 faces 12 edges 24 angles
△ based prism	faces edges angles	5 faces 9 edges 12 angles
measuring angles right angle		the right angle on my roof is 90°. the rightangle on the side of my roof is 90°
acute angle		there are 4 acute angle on my house. the acute angles are 45°
obtuse angle		there are 0 obtuse angles on my house.

L'ESCORIAL   2D

—— JULY 1588 ——

HE MUCKED UP OUR — INVASION PLAN

He Duke of Palma mucked up our invasion plan because he was not ready in Dunkruk to sail.

Philip II was very angry when he found out. On the other hand Philip was pleased with The Duke of Medina Sidenia because he had reached Calais but losing too many ships and not having a sea battle with Englande.

After this achievement, How did the Duke of Palma dare to say that his 17,000 men, 1000 cavalry, 170 ships would not be ready to 2 weeks.

THE GOLDEN HIND   lgr

—— 1st August 1588 ——

ARMADA SIGHTED

It was two weeks ago at south of Eddy-stone Lighthouse that the Armada was spotted by the English Fleet. 1 week ago the English Fleet positioned themselves behind the Spanish Fleet and had the advantage of being windward. A couple of days ago the prize ship. "San Salvardor" arrived at Weymouth badly damaged. We think that there was an explosion below decks. There were quite a few smoke blackened corpses on board.

Fight for Elizabeth
—She is our Queen—

FIRE SHIPS

A plan to send out some fire ships to Calais harbour in France is still to be decided on for Queen Elizabeth is not sure whether it is a good idea.

THE ORANGE
AUG 1589

THE DUTCH LURE

We have been looking at our reports and they say that England ae going to win. We do hope so, when we went to interview Lord Effingham he said they have a good chance of winning. Spains ships are sinking by the hour and about 150 men have been killed. We will continue this story next week.

THE RECORD
AUGUST 14

4D

THE ARMADA

PHILIP OR ELIZABETH There has been months of conflict between England and Spain. Does it really matter to us Scots ? Our contacts inform us that defences have been set up in England, because rumours of the invasion, beacons have been set up in selected areas.
 Rumours of Philips invasion plan have leeked out of Spain, he plans to make Elizabeth 1 pay for the invasion 2 stop helping the Dutch 3 stop killing catholics.

forces of Islam. Indeed there was a permanent Muslim community in London and large numbers of Englishmen could be found in the Middle East and North Africa. The English were close military allies of the Moroccans and the Ottoman Turks: for example there was a joint Anglo-Moroccan attack on Cadiz in 1596.

In 1603 Ahmad al-Manser, the King of Morocco, proposed to Elizabeth I that England should help the Moors to expel their hated Spanish enemies from America and keep the land under joint dominion for ever. He suggested the colonists should be mainly Moroccan, 'in respect of the great heat of the clymat'. Such a proposal, which although finally rejected by Her Majesty, raised few eyebrows at the time, would have completely changed the history of the modern world.

Since 1995 new websites, films and books also provide increased opportunities to consider the different ways in which Tudor times are represented, at a range of levels. The Globe website is one example.

Give reasons for different ways in which the past is represented and interpreted	Compare illustrations of the Globe Theatre in books. Identify evidence for reconstruction of the Globe http://www.reading.ac.uk/globe. The website information to construct our model globe theatre. Perform 'Elizabethan' stick puppet plays.	*Level 3* can identify differences in illustrations.

Level 4 explain how evidence is interpreted for reconstruction

Level 5 suggest why illustrations/your model are different. |

Extracts from the film *Shakespeare in Love* (with its final West Indian beach scene filmed in Norfolk) could stimulate interesting discussions. Children would love to perform Elizabethan scenes from *Blackadder: The Whole Damn Dynasty* (Curtis and Elton 1999). One student had her own thinking about 'interpretations' stimulated by a Year 3 pupil who was enjoying a cartoon story about Francis Drake (Gerrard 1998) and wanted to know why the sixteenth-century portrait painter had not made him 'a little fat man'.

Chapter 5
Collaboration in Professional Development

There has been an increasing emphasis in recent years on developing partnerships between schools and colleges, which are based on clear links between the standards for the award of Qualified Teacher Status (QTS) which underpin courses of Initial Teacher Training (DfEE 1998b) and the support and assessment of trainee teachers in achieving and demonstrating these professional competences in schools. There has also been increased emphasis on literacy, numeracy and ICT which has endangered the position of history in the curriculum. This has led to energetic statements about the importance of history, both in its own right and in relation to other subjects.

Professor Robin Alexander has said that:

> The dominant values underlying Britain's current obsession with literacy and numeracy targets are the same now as in the 1970s, economic instrumentalism, cultural reproduction and social control...as educationalists we have to challenge them...It is a mistake to raise literacy and numeracy standards by downgrading the rest of the curriculum
>
> (*Times Educational Supplement*, 5 December 1997, p. 17)

Even Nicolas Tate, who was at the time Chief Executive of the Qualifications and Curriculum Authority, wrote in *The Times* (14 January 1998), 'No-one in their right mind thinks that simply increasing the amount of time devoted to English and maths will raise standards!'

Christine Counsell, editor of *Teaching History*, said that

> The butcher (Kenneth Clarke), the baker (Kenneth Baker) and the curriculum fudge maker (Sir Ron Dearing) have destroyed carefully worked balances...
>
> (*Times Educational Supplement*, 11 April 1997).

The Historical Association produced a press release (13 January 1998) which, while supporting the aim to increase levels of literacy and numeracy, listed ways in which history develops these skills, by

- introducing and consolidating writing, reading and speaking skills
- encouraging children to read and construct stories of the past
- teaching how different media communicate information and ideas
- expanding vocabulary through rich descriptions of people, places and events
- teaching children the stories behind everyday words
- motivating children to learn basic and advanced study skills
- teaching children skills of chronology and time measurement.

The press release also listed ways in which history contributes to the whole curriculum by

- developing individuals' and collective senses of identity
- exploring the diverse heritage of different cultures and nations
- giving children first-hand experiences of fieldwork in rural and urban environments
- developing knowledge and understanding of other peoples and cultures.

And it showed how history develops a sense of individuality by

- enabling children to read, view and listen critically
- stimulating children's curiosity and imagination
- raising children's awareness of ethical and moral issues
- opening stories of a child's locality, region, nation and world
- giving children a sense of the plurality and diversity of their world
- encouraging children to develop opinions based upon their reason and interpretations of evidence.

The 2000 National Curriculum acknowledges the role of history in a broad, balanced, value-based curriculum and encourages links between history and other subjects, particularly the core subjects. The National Literacy Strategy also states that, while the focus of teaching must be on literacy objectives most of this practice should be linked to other curriculum areas, and that this is fundamental in effective literacy teaching (DfEE 1998a: 13–14). Making these links precisely and effectively, in ways which also focus on the key thinking and learning objectives of each subject, although creative and stimulating, is also a demanding and time-consuming process and it is understandable that teachers' main concern has been to first become confident in using the national strategies for literacy and numeracy discretely, without attempting to link either context or thinking processes to other subjects. As a result children as well as teachers have become familiar with the technical language. As one seven-year-old said with confidence, 'I know all about the literacy hour, skim and scan and similes and menopause'.

This chapter describes case studies in which college tutors and students worked with teachers and children in partnership schools to explore ways in which precise links between history and literacy, history and mathematics and also history, ICT and music could be identified and developed in imaginative ways.

History and the literacy hour: divorce or marriage

It was a shock to find a group of fourth-year history specialist students late in January 2000 state emphatically at the beginning of a session on 'Developing literacy skills through history' that, 'this cannot be done. It is wrong. You must have either history or literacy learning objectives. Everybody says so'. Had they been intimidated by David Blunkett?

> I believe this (literacy) is often taught through other subjects such as history or project work rather than specific lessons. After 1999...the government plans to introduce spot checks by government inspectors on literacy teaching.
> (*The Times* 23 March 1997: 2)

At the end of the session outlined below, when asked who might have a go at making links between history and the literacy hour, the students all said that they would. What a relief! They will have two excellent books to stimulate further ideas, *History and English in the Primary School* (Hoodless 1998), a theoretical examination of a variety of case studies, and *Narrative Matters* (Bage 1999), a scholarly examination of the teaching of history through story. However these books do not make precise links between history and the national literacy framework. The Literacy through History Project at Exeter University (Nichol 1988: Lewis and Wray 1988; Nichol 2000) makes links between a history hour and a literacy hour but consciously attempts to make the literacy hour as discrete as possible. The following sequence of case studies undertaken in 1998, 1999 and 2000 further explores to what extent and how more explicit links can be made.

Kendal Castle 1998

In order to define precise links between learning objectives for history and for English in the National Curriculum, five student teachers worked inten.sively for three days with a Year 1/2 class in Stramongate School, Kendal. They visited Kendal Castle, and found out more about castles from other sources in order, firstly, to create a role-play of what a medieval banquet in Kendal Castle may have been like and, secondly, to make a children's information board for the castle, since they found that the board on the site, written for adults, was difficult for them to understand. This project (Cooper 1997; 1998a; 1998b) preceded the national literacy framework, so it is interesting, though not surprising, that each of the activities had both National Curriculum for History (2000) learning objectives and National Literacy Framework text level objectives (Table 5.1). It could therefore have been taught over a longer period through a sequence of literacy hours.

Table 5.1 Activities with combined National Curriculum History and National Literacy Framework Learning Objectives. Kendal Castle

History NC	NLF

FINDING OUT ABOUT THE CASTLE
2b   Concept Map of Castle
      Identify differences between ways of life
      at different times
	Write captions 1.1.14
	labels for drawings/diagrams 1.2.22
	to explain, describe 1.3.21

4b Questions to investigate about the past . . .	Write simple questions 1.2.24 1.3.22
Site Visit – notes 4a Find out about past from sources. 5 Communicate in writing; drawing.	make simple lists for planning, reminding etc. 1.1.15 assemble information from our experience 1.2.25 use headings; sub-headings 2.3.20

4a.   Inferences from brass-rubbing
      Find out about the past from a range of
      sources
	describe characteristics, behaviour simple
	profiles of characters 1.2.15
	write character profiles, simple descriptions 2.2.14

5.   RECONSTRUCTING A BANQUET IN THE
        CASTLE FROM PRIMARY AND
        SECONDARY SOURCES	

Communicate awareness of the past in different ways; talking, writing, drawing Invitation to banquet	Substitute and extend patterns from reading 1.2.13
Theme for banquet Programme for entertainment	simple lists 1.1.15 organise in lists 1.2.25 read for information and record answers 1.3.22 use models from reading to organise sequentially 2.1.16 make simple notes from non-fiction texts 2.3.19
Story for banquet: Sleeping Beauty The banquet	use patterned stories as models using basic conventions 1.1.10 represent outlines of story plots 1.2.14 write stories, based on reading 1.3.14 use the language of time 2.1.11 use the language of story . . . 2.3.10
Use primary and secondary sources to ask and answer questions about the past; communicate information: The kitchen Plan	Simple non-chronological reports 1.2.25 using language of texts read as models for 1.3.20 writing 2.3.21 use diagrams drawing, labelling 2.1.17 instructions 2.2.19

First the children were asked to 'draw and label a picture of a castle: the ideas that come into your head when someone says "castle". Students scribed for younger children. This was in order to find out what children already knew (and possible misconceptions); what images they had of castles. Some children had a lot of factual knowledge, about moats, drawbridges, arrow-slits; others were dominated by fantasy – garlands of flowers around the turrets; Max, from *Where the Wild Things Are* in a boat on a rescue mission across the moat (Sendak 1970).

Then the class were told that they were visiting Kendal Castle in the afternoon and asked what they would like to find out about it. Their questions were listed on a flip-chart and grouped into four focuses:

- now and then: what can you see from the castle mound now and what would you have seen a long time ago – certainly; possibly?
- attacking the castle: why was it built here; how could you attack? where?
- daily life: where did they cook; wash; get water, have banquets?
- survey of the site: measure curtain wall, windows, doorways; note materials, where did they come from?

In the afternoon the children worked in groups on the site to record information in notes and lists. Some children organised their notes under headings, others recorded as small drawings, with labels scribed for them where necessary.

Next day preparations began to reconstruct a banquet at Kendal Castle in the time of Catherine Parr, who had lived there as a child. In order to find out how to dress, children made rubbings of replica medieval brasses, including one of Catherine Parr. This gave them lots of information about ladies' headdresses, 'belts with tassels', patterns on dresses; about knights' chain mail, armour, helmets, swords, coats of arms on shields. Then each child chose a small item of dress from their rubbing, a necklace or a shield, for example, and made a replica, from card, fabric or shiny paper, which they could wear to the banquet.

They found the rest of the information they needed to plan the banquet from books – usually from illustrations, either artists' reconstructions or contemporary pictures. *The Medieval Cookbook* (Black 1992), although an adult book, has splendidly vivid pictures of medieval feasts to accompany the recipes: killing the boar, baking the bread, roasting birds on spits etc. Invitations were sent (modelled on familiar party invitations), menus were written and programmes for entertainment devised. These were divided into sub-headings; during the meal – stories, jesting, lute – and after the meal – singing, jesters, dancing and tournaments. Samantha's drawing of the joust (Figure 5.1) and accompanying writing (Figure 5.2) show how the interpretation of medieval people on the brasses was brought to life by her further enquiry using information book illustrations of knights, which informed the joust role-play following the

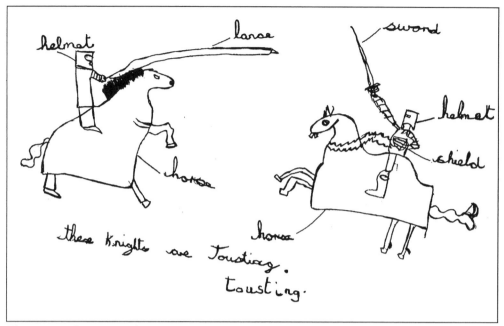

Figure 5.1 Samantha found out about jousting from information books

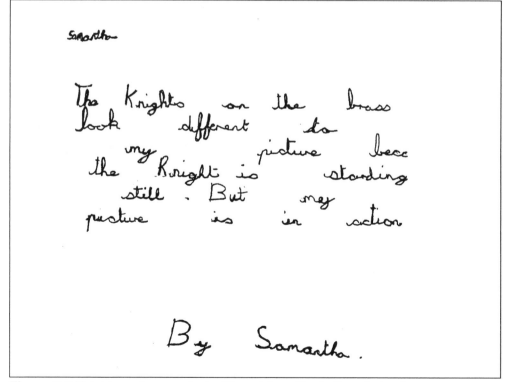

Figure 5.2 Knights on brasses look different from illustrations in books

banquet. Stories were written, to be read during the meal, modelled on the familiar conventions of fairy stories about princes and princesses. Jokes were remodelled suitably for medieval jesters: why did the chicken cross the drawbridge? Replica food was prepared (finding from their researches that squirrels were eaten, as well as boars' heads, a lugubrious pig's head and some surprisingly perky-looking squirrels were carried to the table with great care on a large silver salver). Following the banquet jugglers caught most of the balls, everyone laughed at the jesters' riddles, and Baron Dorset, looking remarkably like the head teacher, joined in the dancing to the viol, the harp and the crumhorn of the Past Times tape.

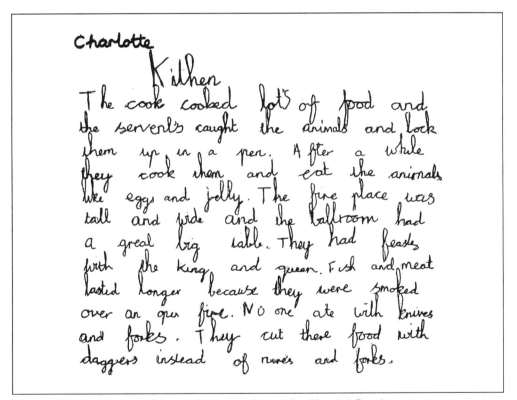

Figure 5.3 Children made an information board for Kendal Castle

The various examples of non-chronological writing on the children's information board (Figure 5.3) were an excellent assessment of the enormous range of detailed information the children had a acquired over the intensive three-day project and the site plan of Kendal Castle, with its topographically accurate key to the plan of the castle, showed a significant development from the fairy-tale fantasy castles of the initial concept maps to a factual labelled diagram.

If this project were repeated as a series of literacy hours the sessions may be structured differently, with planned work at word and sentence level, more explicit emphasis on modelling the story, jokes, invitations, menus, and on analysing the characteristic features and purposes of captions, labels, notes, diagrams. The literacy objectives might be made more explicit, but certainly the motivation to do the work would be intrinsic, rather than as with some literacy hours, a collection of discrete exercises. This case study is a good example of the way in which the literacy framework makes more explicit, but does not change, the National Curriculum for English.

Abbot Hall Museum, Kendal (1999)

The following year another group of students, Alex, Alison, Sarra, Suzanne and Laura, volunteered to work on a two-day project in Stramongate School to investigate how more precise links could be made between history learning objectives and the literacy hour (Cooper and Twiselton 1998; 1999). Both Year 2 and Year 5 were studying the Victorians and were going to visit Abbot Hall Museum in Kendal where rooms are furnished as a nineteenth-century bedroom and kitchen. It was decided that the focus of the literacy hours for both classes would be the museum visits in order to see how museum work on artefacts could be linked to the literacy framework at two different levels. 'Alphabets' was chosen as a theme for the museum visits for several reasons. Learning the alphabet by rote was a key feature of Victorian Board schools, and alphabet books were written for middle-class children to read at home. Both provide opportunities for discussing phonics and phonemes, for using patterning, rhythm, rhyme and picture clues to predict meaning; for shared reading; for modelling writing. They provide opportunities for discussing the meaning of archaic words such as vintner, squire and oyster-wench. The three alphabets selected also reflected changes in attitudes to children over the century. 'A was an Archer' (in Opie and Opie 1980) made few concessions to childhood; Kate Greenaway (Ernest 1968) romanticised it; Edward Lear (Sampson 1977; Alderson 1975) enjoyed it!

The literacy hours were supported by a variety of history-focused activities. The reasons for attempting to make links between the literacy hours and the history topic were firstly, to create curriculum coherence and secondly to give the literacy hour activities a purpose and an audience. However the conclusion reached at the end of this case study was that although literacy hours may sometimes meet history objectives their focus must be on literacy.

The project began, for each class (at different times) with the visit to Abbot Hall Museum, where the children were shown an amazing, hand-painted cloth alphabet book, made by a Kendal woman, Mrs Clara Walker, for her two-year old daughter Mary in 1891, and photographs of Mrs Walker and Mary. 'What is this?' they were asked, 'Who made it? How? Why?' After reading and marvelling at Mrs Walker's book they were asked the same questions about other intriguing Victorian artefacts set out on the tables: butter pats, bellows, curling tongs etc. Then the Year 2 children were divided into five groups. Each group was given five (non-consecutive) letters of the alphabet and asked to list as many artefacts as they could find in the bedroom and kitchen beginning with 'their' letters. This was made easier by the labels on many artefacts and competition was fierce. 'I've got 10 – 23 – 30'. 'Does cast-iron cauldron count for two?' 'If you say ragged rag-rug is that three?'

Literacy Hour (Year 2, Term 2)
Whole class: text level
Learning objectives: to reinforce word level skills (T1); use phonological contextual grammatical and graphic knowledge to check and predict meanings of unfamiliar words (T2); identify and discuss patterns of rhythm and rhyme (T9). ·

After discussing the cloth alphabet book they had seen in the morning, Alex showed the children a printed version of an old alphabet book, *The Nursery Companion* (Opie and Opie 1980), to give them some more ideas about how they could make their own Victorian alphabet book. They began reading 'A was an Archer' together.

> A was an Archer
> And shot at a frog
> B was a butcher
> And kept a great dog...

Alliteration, similar sentence structure, rhyme, rhythm and pictures all helped to predict the meaning of unfamiliar language: nobleman, tinker, watchman.

Whole class: word level
Learning objectives: identify phonemes in speech and writing (W2); apply phonological and graphic knowledge, through guided writing.

After more explicit discussion at word level Alex wrote the alphabet on a flip-chart and helped the children to put the names on 'their' artefacts, seen in the museum with 'their' letter, discussing spellings as she did so.

Independent group work
Learning objectives: to identify phonemes in speech and writing (W2); secure use of simple sentences in writing (S9).

The children wrote simple sentences, modelling those on the flip-chart for 'their' artefacts, e.g. D is for dolly tub, with the potential for an explanatory clause, 'for washing the clothes'.

Guided group (Alison)
Learning objectives: common spelling patterns (W2); split familiar words into component parts (W4); use structures from poems as a basis for writing (T15); comment on and recognise when reading a poem aloud is effective.

This group read and were captivated by the rhyming pattern of the Lear alphabet – a pattern which was nonsense but followed conventions. They used their artefact words to construct nonsense alphabet entries, an interesting way of looking at patterns and exceptions in the meanings, sounds and visual appearance of words.

> Bottle
> Tottle
> Mottle
> Gottle
> Jottle
> Big blue medicine bottle

Plenary
Learning objectives: read own poems aloud (T8); comment on and recognise when reading aloud makes sense and is effective (T10).

The children read their poems and alphabet entries in order. They recorded their work on tape. As a postscript many chose to redraft their efforts for a second recording later in the day, accentuating the alliteration and rhythm they could hear in the first recording. This version was illustrated and collated into the children's own 'Victorian Alphabet Book'.

Literacy Hour 2
The following literacy hour followed the theme of pattern and rhythm, in Victorian street cries, using the *Victorians, Music from the Past*, text and audio tape (Longman 1987).

Whole class: text level
Learning objectives: identify and discuss patterns of rhythm, rhyme and other features of sound in different poems (T).

After playing a tape of Victorian street chants, Alex led a discussion building up a vivid picture of a Victorian market scene and the use of chants to sell goods. She talked about the need for the chants to be memorable and easy to repeat, making use of rhythm, rhyme and snappy slogans to do this.

Whole class: word and text level
Learning objectives: discriminate orally syllables in multi-syllabic words (W5); comment on and recognise when the reading aloud of a poem makes sense and is effective (T10); use structures from poems as a basis for writing (T15).

The class read the street cries together, looking for rhymes first, and underlining them, before focusing on the rhythm. They also made up their own market chants (based on their letters) orally, which were then written down.

Group work
(W5; T10; T15)
The children were each given a chant and worked in pairs, tapping out the rhythm of their given chant with a pencil. They tried doing the various chants as a round, before constructing their own. There was discussion of the use of speech marks, exclamation marks and question marks, which they employed effectively in their writings.

Plenary session
Learning objectives: read own poem aloud (T8); comment on and recognise when the reading aloud of a poem makes sense and is effective (T10).

The children performed their street chants to each other, with discussion of what made them effective.

More Victorians

Work in the literacy hour in Year 2 was linked to a rich variety of other history-focused activities, planned by the students. One group used photographs of a Victorian parlour, a family living in one room, a school and an ironmonger's shop. They were given a sheet of A1 paper divided into four boxes and tried to find clues to differences between now and then for each box. In the ironmonger's box they wrote 'the packaging was darker than today's', and 'customers had to ask for things then. Today we don't'.

One group found out more about artefacts borrowed from Abbot Hall in order to label them for a class museum. Greg found out about button hooks. 'Gaiters have a sort of key with a hook on the end, and a hole at the end to put your thigh in.'

Some children coloured (photocopied) line drawings from Kate Greenaway's *Colouring Book*, imitating her delicate colours and writing interpretations of the pictures. 'They're collecting flowers to sell at the market.' 'It's lavender to make lavender bags.' 'They're wild flowers.' Others followed instructions to make Victorian peg dolls, then made up a 'Victorian story' which they wrote in tiny books, like the miniature books they had seen inside Kate Greenaway's *Treasury*. The peg dolls acted out the story.

Another group made a replica Pollock's theatre, like the one the student had bought in Pollock's Toy Museum and decided to write and perform the story of the Minotaur.

Year 5, Term 2

When Year 5 visited Abbot Hall they also discussed Mrs Walker's cloth alphabet book and artefacts in the handling collection, but they were encouraged to use conditional language (if, then, should, might) and conjunctions (and, but). 'If you had an ostrich feather fan, you might have been rich, because ostrich feathers had to be imported, but the feathers might have been more common then!' Then each child was given one letter and asked to find an artefact in the museum beginning with their letter, draw it and write notes describing it and explaining how it worked, how it was made, who might have used it and why.

Literacy Hour, Year 5, Term 2

Whole class: text level

Learning objectives: locate information confidently and efficiently through (i) using indexes/headings (ii) skimming (iii) scanning (iv) close reading (T17).

After an introductory look at 'A was an Archer', the Victorian alphabet (in Opie and Opie 1980) Suzanne contrasted this with a modern dictionary to establish what children already knew about dictionaries. It was explained that they were going to write a dictionary of Victorian artefacts. They were then given photocopied pages from a variety of modern dictionaries and discussed definitions, and the use of abbreviations to denote nouns, verbs, adverbs and plurals.

Whole class: word level

Learning objectives: use dictionaries (W3); search for, collect and define technical words (W9) evaluate text critically by comparing how different sources treat the same information (T18).

Suzanne explained that not all dictionaries have so much information, and she asked for feedback from the children on what was in the different dictionaries in front of them. This led to a series of dictionary games where words were suggested and children had to race to locate them and find all the information on them available in the dictionary they had.

Group/Individual work

Learning objectives: to convert personal notes into notes for others to read, paying attention to appropriateness of style, vocabulary, presentation (T21); search for, collect and define technical words (W9);

The children were asked to write dictionary entries for artefacts they had drawn and written notes on in the museum.

Plenary
Definitions were read and evaluated.

In the second literacy hour Laura and the class read Edward Lear's *A Book of Bosh* (Alderson 1975) together, then discussed the ways in which this was a shift from the other more literal Victorian alphabets. They noticed the difficulties of reading alliteration at speed. (It was explained that they were going to write their own Victorian 'Book of Bosh'.) For word and sentence level work they chose the letter P and wrote as many words as they could think of beginning with P on separate cards, then tried to make sentences with them, rearranging and substituting them. Then they worked in pairs. Each pair was given a pile of blank cards and asked to experiment with 'bosh' sentences about the Victorian artefacts they had drawn in the museum, constructing them in different ways by reordering (S8), then writing in a final form (T13).

In the plenary children enjoyed listening to and making constructive comments on each others' efforts (T24).

Flighty footmen fancied feather-fans...

Even more Victorians
To consolidate what else they knew about the Victorians, the Year 6 children worked in groups to construct spider diagrams about photographs of Victorian subjects – a parlour, a shop, a beach, for example – showing ways in which life in Victorian times was different from today and suggesting why. When they shared their diagrams they found that each group had organised their analyses in quite different ways, creating a variety of 'spiders'.

In one session children studied photocopies of Victorian illuminated letters. The class then made their own Victorian illuminated letters. Half of them used scraps of fabric, velvet, silk, lace, beads, as this was identified in one of the pattern books as a popular early Victorian pastime. These contrasted with the cardboard prints of birds, leaves, fruits and vines inspired by William Morris designs which the rest of the class made as a background for their superimposed letters. This was an interesting example of using historical sources to illustrate how patterns, colours and textures reflected changes in nineteenth-century design.

In another intense session children used information books to find out about aspects of Victorian schools: reading, writing and arithmetic; drill; playground games. As a class they decided on four key words for each topic; in groups they were given 20 minutes in pairs to list questions related to each set of key words and try to find out the answers.

Then, each group worked on a short role-play on their topic, using these facts (History KE3, 4 a, g; English 2c). Tables were recited and very hard arithmetic problems were posed, to which only the inspector knew the answer, probably because 's' (shillings) and 'd' (pence) were incomprehensible (but, like his Victorian counterpart, the inspector had an answer book). Drill was rigorous. At playtime 'The Big Ship Sailed up the Alley Alley O'; and of course the alphabet, chanted and painstakingly copied onto slates, played a major part in the reading and writing lessons. Dunces were reprimanded; and certificates were awarded for graphic and phonic skills, and for definitions of 'Gradgrind' accuracy: 'K is for kettle; noun; made of metal; hangs over the fire; used to warm water'.

Role-play – A Victorian street, with a school on one side and a grand family house on the other (English AT 1 a-c; History KE3, 5c).

On the third afternoon, the Year 2 and Year 5 classes waited quietly, facing each other in the hall, to share what they had learned about the Victorians. A hunched figure, barefoot and enveloped in a vast paisley shawl, walked between them. She had a strange accent. She seemed to think she was in a London street. She said she could see a tall, grey building on one side of it – 'A three-decker, big high windows – it must be one of them new schools'. She peered inside. 'Can you see all the children inside? I thought you could; you've got magic eyes like me – cor – innit strict?'

Everybody suspended disbelief and looked in turn at the various activities going on in the school. Then they all agreed that on the other side of the street they could see a grand house, with its brass knocker and railings and red velvet curtains. They could even peep into the parlour where the children were performing a puppet play, Theseus and the Minotaur. A peg-doll play about Queen Victoria was then presented by the children in the big house.

Following this, the cries of street sellers were heard approaching – some cries were familiar; others were new.

> White tur-nips, white, young tur-nips white!
> Fine car-rots O! Fine car-rots O!

Then

> Red raspberries red, fresh raspberries red!
> Clothes, clothes, any old clothes?

And

> Who'll buy my sweet, red roses
> So fresh and sweet as night?
> Who'll buy my hot spiced gingerbread?
> Smoking hot and good to eat?

Then a sweet-seller appeared.

> Jelly beans, liquorice, who'll buy my liquorice?

Everyone was rewarded.

Can history and literacy objectives be achieved within the literacy hour? (2000)

The cohort of history specialist students who met in January 2000 listened to accounts of the case studies undertaken by their predecessors. In the first there had been concurrent National Curriculum and literacy objectives but not within the literacy hour format. In the second the literacy objectives dominated the literacy hours but these linked by content to the history activities of the study unit on the Victorians. The challenge for the students in this workshop was to explore ways in which history and literacy objectives might both be an integral part of a literacy hour. The focus was on reading and writing non-fiction from Reception to Year 6. Each group of students was given a text and a list of pre-selected history objectives and literacy hour objectives at text, sentence and word level for a given year and term and asked to draft a literacy hour plan combining as many of the objectives as possible. The plans they produced could be translated into a variety of other contexts. Here are some examples.

Finding out about Victorian washday: reading and writing instructional text at Year 2, Term 1

This could be applied to explaining how any artefact was used.

History Objectives

1b   Use common words or phrases related to passing of time.
2b   Identify differences between ways of life at different times.
4a   Find out about the past from a range of sources.
5   Communicate awareness and knowledge of history.

Literacy Hour Objectives
Text level
T13   Read simple instructions.
T14   Note structured features: statement of purpose at start, sequential steps in list; direct language.
T15   Write simple instructions.
T16   Organise sequentially (lists, numbers) each point depending on the previous one.
T18   Use appropriate register (direct; impersonal).

Sentence level
   Reread own writing for sense and punctuation.
   Use simple organisational devised to indicate sequence (arrows), boxes, keys.

Word level
New words linked to particular topics.

Victorian washday: literacy hour plan (Year 2, Term 1)
Whole class: text level
Show wash tub, scrubbing board, postle, iron, line, pegs, soap.
H1b • What were these things used for? When?
H2b • Why? What do we use today?
H4a • By whom? Who does the washing today?
H4b • How do you think the scrubbing board was used? Can you follow Mrs
       Tiggy Winkle's washing instructions?

       To Wash a Shirt
       You will need:
       • A scrubbing board
       • A wash tub
       • Hot water
       • Soap
       Half-fill wash tub with hot water
       Put in dirty clothes
       Stand scrubbing board in the wash tub
       Stretch dirty shirt across scrubbing board
       Rub the shirt with soap until it is clean
       Wring out soapy water
       Rinse the shirt in clean water
       Hang on outdoor clothes line to dry with pegs, or on clothes' horse by
       kitchen fire, it if is raining.

T13 • Child mimes as instructions are read from flip-chart (or overhead
       transparency).
T18 • Were they good instructions? Why?
       Identify   * statement of purpose
                  * sequential steps; each point depends on previous one
                  * direct impersonal language.

Whole class: word level
T10 • Do you know what the other things are called? (label)
     • How do you think you use the postle?
     • Child mimes as class read scrubbing board instructions, changing as
       necessary for postle.
     • Explain class are going to make a book of Mrs Tiggy Winkle's washing
       instructions.

Independent groups

T15   • You are going to write instructions for using the postle.
T16   • Either write the instructions as for the scrubbing board, or draw pictures or a diagram with labels.
      Remember: purpose, sequence, register.

Focus group

T15   • We are going to explain how to use a flat iron (key instructional features, but new information).

Plenary

S4   • Read instructions for using postle and iron; child mimes.

H5   • Evaluate for inclusion in Mrs Tiggy Winkle's washday book.

What were Ancient Egyptian houses like? Year 4, Term 2

This model could be used to find out about a key aspect of any area of study from a variety of reference books.

History Objectives

H4a,b Asking and answering questions about the past, using variety of sources.
H3   Understanding why there are different interpretations of the past.

Literacy Hour Objectives
Text level

T15   Appraise a non-fiction book for its contents and usefulness by scanning (e.g. headings, contents list).
T16   To prepare for factual research by reviewing what is known, what is available and where one might search.
T17   To scan text in print or on screen to locate key words or phrases, useful headings and key questions and to use these as a tool for summarising text.
T18   Mark extracts by annotating and by selecting key headings, words, sentences.
T20   Identify key features of explanatory text (e.g. to answer a question, use of illustrations and diagrams).

Sentence level

1   Use cues (phonic, graphic, grammatical knowledge, context when reading unfamiliar texts).
2   Understand that vocabulary changes over time (e.g. discuss why some words have become little used).

Egyptian houses: literacy hour plan (Year 4, Term 2)

Whole class: text level

Show OHT photocopy of a page about an Ancient Egyptian house from a reference book.

T16   What do you already know about houses in Ancient Egypt?

H4a,b   How can we find out more? (Archaeological remains, tomb, book.)
        The information in books comes from making deductions and inferences about archaeological sources; different books may say different things. We are going to see what we can find out from these books: what is the same/different; how useful the books are.

T15   Where can we find out about Egyptian houses in this book? (Contents, index.) Find text.

T17   Read page (an OHT).

T18   Mark key information. List on flip-chart under headings.

T20   Discuss usefulness of text, illustrations, diagrams.

Whole class: sentence level

S1   Discuss unfamiliar vocabulary: brewery, bakery, silo, granary.

S11   Do we still use these words today? When? How has their meaning remained the same/changed?

Independent group work

Groups given other reference books at appropriately differentiated levels.

T15   Find reference to Egyptian houses.

T21   List key words/information.

Plenary

T23   Whole class list what they have found out on flip-chart, adding under original headings.

H4   Note differences between books; discuss reasons.

T24   Reorganise list under headings, sub-headings, numbered points.

Hilaire Bellocs' Cautionary Tales. Matilda, Who Told Lies and was Burned to Death (1991). Humorous verse, Year 3, Term 3

History Objectives

H2a,b   Characteristic features of period and experiences of middle-class child.

H4   Find out about the past from a variety of sources.
        Discuss clues in illustrations about when poem written:
        – tea in the drawing room – servants.

About Matilda's life:
- fire engine
- street scenes
- clothes
- carriages.

Literacy Hour Objectives

T4   Consider credibility of events.

T6   Discuss character behaviour.

Text level

T6   Compare forms of humour, e.g. cautionary tales.

T7   Prepare, read aloud and recite by heart, poetry that plays with language or entertains; recognise rhyme and patterns of sound that create effects.

T8   Compare and contrast works by the same author.

Sentence level

S4   Use speech marks and other dialogue punctuation.

Word level

W4   Discriminate syllables in reading and spelling.

W12 Collect new words from reading and work in other subjects.

Matilda: literacy hour plan (Year 3, Term 3)

Whole class: text level

T4   Read poem: what is it about? Is it likely? True?

T5   Is Matilda reasonable? Brave? Foolish?

H4 T6 Discuss clues in illustrations about Matilda and her life; similarities with and differences from children today. Introduce concept of 'cautionary tales'.

T7   What makes it fun? Identify rhythm. Mark a photocopied page (OHTs).

T8   Introduce other Belloc cautionary tales to read at another time.

Whole class: sentence level

S4   Identify speech and punctuation marks: 'Matilda's house is burning down!' using photocopied page (OHT).
        They only answered 'little liar'.

Whole class: word level

W4   Tap out syllables (using OHT page).

W12   Reread. List any new words (e.g. gallant, frenzied).

Independent/group work

W4

T7   Give children photocopied pages to read; to mark rhymes; syllables; prepare to recite.

Guided group work

T15   Give children sheets marked with lines of eight dashes (one per syllable). Help them make up their own, modern, cautionary verse.

Plenary

T1   Class recite their pages, to read complete poem in sequence. Guided group read their poem. H2d T2 Discuss what makes them effective. How is Victorian poem the same/different from modern version?

Advertisements

Persuasive Text. Year 4, Term 3.

Commercial advertisements can be read as an historical source. They both mirror and influence the ways of life, aspirations and social values of men, women, children and the ways in which these change from decade to decade. Children are familiar with the concepts of advertising and can understand them as persuasive interpretations. Text is minimal, supported by clear picture clues and illustrates a range of linguistic features. The History of Advertising Trust is an excellent resource (www.hatads.org.uk): posters for whole-class work; calendars which children can work on individually or in groups. Their collection on 'Women in Advertising – from Victorian Times to Today' was used to plan for the following learning objectives.

History Objectives

H4a,b Ask and answer questions from sources about life in the 1890s; 1930 to the present.

H2a   Characteristics of periods and societies, attitudes and experiences of men, women, children.

H2b   Social diversity.

H2c   Reasons for situations and changes.

H2d   Make links between situations, changes, within and across periods.

Reasons why the past is represented and interpreted in different ways.

Literacy Hour Objectives

T18   From examples of persuasive writing investigate how style and vocabulary can be used to convince the intended reader.

T19   To evaluate advertisements for impact, appeal, honesty, focusing on how information about the product is presented: exaggerated claims, tactics for grabbing attention, linguistic devises; puns, jingles, alliteration, invented words.

T25   To design an advertisement making use of linguistic and other features learned from examples.

S3   To understand how the grammar of a sentence is altered; statement to question; question to order; positive to negative.

W15   To use a range of presentational skills, e.g. print script for captions, headings for posters, range of computer-generated fonts.

The opportunities to use these skills in order to discuss and evaluate messages of old advertisements, and compare them with those of today offer an exciting variety of possibilities.

Diary of Anne Frank (21 August 1942) (OHT)
Diaries and journals recounting experiences and events (Year 6, Term 1).

History Objectives

H4   Find out about the past from a variety of sources.

H2a,b About characteristic features of periods and beliefs, attitudes and experiences of men, women and children; about social, religious, cultural, ethnic diversity.

Literacy Hour Objectives

T3   Personal responses to literature, identifying why and how a text affects the reader. Prepare a short section of the story as a script.

T11   Distinguish between biography and autobiography, fact and opinion, implicit and explicit point of view.

T14   Develop skills of biographical and autobiographical writing in role of an historical character through describing a person from different perspectives, e.g. police.

T15   Develop a journalistic style; consider balanced ethical reporting.

S4   Identify connectives to convey sequence; causal connectives.

Anne Frank: literacy hour plan (Year 6, Term 1)
Whole class: text level

H2a,b What do you know about Ann Frank? Put diary extract in context; use website, photo scrap book of story of her life, brief history of the Holocaust, and tour of the rooms where she lived (http://www.annefrank.com).

H4a   Read diary entry.

H4B   What more does this extract tell us (weather, hiding place, holiday ...)?

T11   What is special about a diary (not written for others; personal views, feelings, perspective, language)? What does it tell us about Ann's feelings, relationships, what sort of person she is?

S4   How does Anne explain the time sequence (first three days, now, at present, already, now).
        Identify causal connectives: (because a lot of houses had been searched; because we all knocked ourselves in the doorway).

T15   List on flip-chart what you would need to consider in writing:
        • a newspaper article about the discovery of the diary
        • a police account of search for the hiding place.

Independent group work

HSa,b,c (i) Write a newspaper account of the discovery of the diary.
T14   (ii) Write a police report on searching for the hiding place.
T3   (iii) Read/write another entry from Anne's diary.

Guided group work

H5a,b,c   Prepare a diary extract as a film script.

Plenary

H3 Compare interpretations; discuss fact/opinion; point of view, validity.

After sharing these literacy hour plans, which used a variety of texts across a wide age range, and encompassed both literacy and history objectives, the students agreed that they would have a go at developing these models in other contexts during their coming block placements in schools.

Analysis of links between the National Literacy Strategy and historical thinking

The UK School Museums Group Conference (1999) invited a short paper on links between history and the literacy strategy, which they could use to ensure that discussions of their artefact collections with primary school children and the information labels, brochures and follow-up activities which they provide (quizzes, trails, worksheets) reflect and develop the objectives of the literacy framework. They felt that this would enable them to justify to schools the time spent on visits to museums; a parlous situation – but an interesting exercise. The resulting analysis could also be used as a starting point for developing similar links in school.

Types of non-fiction texts

The summary of the range of non-fiction given in *The National Literacy Strategy Framework* (DfEE 1998a: 66–72) lists a variety of types of text which can be used in historical contexts, and which move from simple description and instruction in Year 1 to discussion and debate in Years 4 to 6.

Information texts

	Y1	Y2	Y3	Y4	Y5	Y6
Signs, labels, captions, lists	Y1					
Non-chronological reports	Y1	Y2	Y3	Y4		Y6
Observations	Y1		Y3	Y4	Y5	
Reports, articles	Y1		Y3	Y4		
Describe and classify				Y4	Y5	
Formal writing: public information, documents etc.						Y6

Instructional texts

	Y1	Y2	Y3	Y4	Y5	Y6
Instructions	Y1	Y2	Y3			
Rules, recipes, directions, instructions showing how things are done						
Processes, systems, operations					Y5	
Explanations		Y2		Y4		Y6
Puzzles, riddles			Y3			
Viewpoints, fact/opinion, discussion, debate				Y4	Y5	

Discussion texts Y6

Chronological texts

	Y1	Y2	Y3	Y4	Y5	Y6
Recount events, activities (visits)					Y5	
Observations which recount experiences over time						Y6

Technical vocabulary

The technical terms which should form part of pupils' developing vocabulary for talking about language (DfEE 1998a: 69–77) can be used in the discussion of and writing about artefacts or other historical sources. Again these develop from simple questions and instructions, an old recipe, how to play a simple Victorian game or use a butter pat at Key Stage 1, to the language of probability, opinion and argument in Year 4 and of hypothesis and perspective in Year 6.

Y1   Question, label, instruction, list, non-chronological writing.

Y2   Explanation, fact, notes, skim, scan.

Y3   Definition, bullet points, past tense, legend, myth.
      Conjunction: if, so, while, though, since, when
          time – first, then, after, meanwhile (Y3, T3, sentence level 5)

Y4   Connection: conditional – 'if … then'; 'on the other hand'; … 'finally'; 'so'
      (Y4, T3, sentence level 4)
      Argument

Debate
Discussion – argument for and against
Opinion
Y5   Chronological sequence
Point of view
Y6   Word derivation
Hypothesis
Viewpoint

Sight vocabulary, writing and spelling

The same pattern is embedded in the high frequency vocabulary children are expected to learn to recognise in context, through shared work, practice and exploration from Reception to Year 2, and to learn to use, write and spell correctly in Years 4/5 (DfEE 1998a: 60–3). These words, with which children are expected to become very familiar, reflect the key questions, deductions and inferences of historical enquiry in increasingly complex ways.

Questions, Deductions and Inferences	R – Y2 Sight recognition	Y4 – 5 Write and spell correctly
Key Questions What is it? How was it made? Used? What did it mean to the people who made/used it?	What Where Who People, their Make, made Name House, home	Used
Probability Distinguish between what is known, possible, probable; Hypotheses	If May Or Should Would	Almost Know, knew Why Think, thought Might Sometimes Sure
Explanations, Opinion	Because So	
Chronology, Change Similarity/difference, cause/effect	After, again, just, last, new, now, next, old, once, then, time, when	Always, before, began between, change, different, during, first, follow(ing), often, still, stopped, suddenly, through, today, while, year

Scaffolding children's historical thinking

Bruner's notion (1966) of devising scaffolding frameworks for supporting and developing children's thinking processes has been applied to thinking in history through research (see Chapter 6, p. 141) and in published history resources (Counsell and Thomson 1997). The National Literacy Strategy has generated many further examples (e.g. Wray and Medwell 1998). Many of these writing frames can be used to enable children to develop the literacy skills defined in the technical vocabulary in historical contexts.

Children can use them to write structured reports about artefacts or sites; this report is about...; detail a, b, c, d; conclusion. They can write explanations of historical events, or of why people in the past may have behaved in a certain way: I want to explain why: reason i) ii) iii) iv); so now you see why...They can use a series of steps to sequence instructions ranging from how to make a peg doll to how to navigate a course to the East Indies in an Elizabethan ship. They can use a template to identify an issue, list arguments for/against, and write a conclusion. If the writing frames are linked to ICT this allows the flexibility to reorganise text, to work collaboratively, and it gives a structure for comparing responses.

Literacy, history and art

A recent exploration of precise ways in which the literacy hour could be linked to an art topic provided even further insights into the possibilities of creative cross-curricular links (Cooper and Twiselton, 2000). This focused on the Impressionists and explored ways in which an art gallery poster could model a range of types of non-fiction text as a basis for whole-class work in the literacy hour. Related group work is supported by four information booklets linked to the (fictional) gallery: explaining the movement and its painters; exploring contrasting views in contemporary newspaper reviews of their exhibitions, the artists' letters and diaries; instructional workshops for learning their techniques; and an information booklet on the gallery and its facilities. These can be used as models for creating similar materials for a class exhibition or display, or gallery visit. Although the focus is on Impressionist painters, the materials could be modified to relate to art from any other period, or to a museum visit, or to model and create different kinds of information text about a class art gallery or museum, through a sequence of literacy hours.

History, the literacy hour and fiction

There has recently been a renewed exploration of ways in which story and in particular fiction set in the past can help children to develop historical understanding (Hoodless 1998; English Heritage 1998a; Bage 1999). When a group of Year 3 BA QTS students worked in pairs on the National Literacy Strategy Summary of Fiction and Poetry (DfEE 1998a: 66–8), brainstorming texts they had actually used, they found that between them they had already used each of the genres specified for each year group in their history teaching. One interesting fact to emerge was that all kinds of historical texts and genres had been adapted for use at a range of levels: the Year 1 spidergraph for example recorded that five-year-old children taught by these students had worked on Egyptian and Greek myths and legends, Saxon and Viking sagas and Chaucer. Year 6 children had worked on extracts from Dickens, Leon Garfield and Rosemary Sutcliffe and written their own scripts after hot-seating as factory owners and child workers.

One student, Hannah Dewfall, said that 'it was my own delight in historical fiction that fuelled my enjoyment of history'. But she was also aware of the dilemmas of teaching history through fiction.

> While English teachers often see historical fiction as a minor genre history teachers often see it as an inaccurate view of historical events. If an historical novel is to be used to teach history, social conditions and public events must be thoroughly researched, free from anachronisms and an integral part of the text.

She went on to explore ways in which literacy hour objectives for fiction might deepen children's historical understanding. Her Year 5 class were reading *The Machine Gunners* (Westall 1975). She focused on two statements to discuss how the central character, a child, is presented through dialogue, action and description and how the reader responds to him through examining his relationship with the other characters (NLS Year 5, Term 1, Text 3).

> Chas watched them as if they were ants, without sympathy, because they were a slummy kind of family.

and

> Besides the dead German would scare the silly little cow. She wouldn't interfere in men's business again.

She used these statements to help the children discuss reasons for attitudes to class, race and gender now and in the past, and why these might change over time.

Another student read extracts from three stories about World War II. *Rose Blanche* (McEwan 1985) a fictional story about concentration camps, *After the War is Over* (Foreman 1995) a story about real children and events in the history of a village and the *Diary of Anne Frank* (Frank 1989), an eyewitness account.

Through focused discussions her Year 6 children considered how the authors handled time and conveyed the passing of time, and the influence of the viewpoint of narrators on the readers' view of events as well as differences between fact, opinion and fiction (Year 5, Term 1, Text 2; 11; Term 2, Text 1); we need such creative teachers who are proactive in responding to change and interpreting requirements in ways which give them ownership and reflect their professional judgements. We do not want passive, mechanistic teachers who are targets for political manipulation. We need literacy to be taught not by teachers who enable children to read, write and cipher by rule and recipe but in ways which provide children with new tools for thinking.

History and the numeracy hour

While the key learning objectives of the numeracy hour must clearly be to develop confidence and competence in mathematics it is often possible to do this in the context of an historical topic. The concepts of measurement, scale and the properties of 2D and 3D shapes could be taught by making and describing models through a sequence of structured numeracy hours (National Numeracy Strategy 6, DfEE 1999a: 102–5). Key Stage 1 work on counting, sets, number sequences in relation to money and real-life problems could be linked to role-play on Victorian market sellers (NNS 5: 2, 4, 6).

Mike and Edward, both aged six, devised their street cry in a literacy hour on victorian street cries (p. 122) but might equally well have done so in a numeracy hour (see Figure 5.4).

Oranges, oranges, roll up, oranges
5p for 1, 10p for 2, 15p for 3, 20p for 4, 5 for 25p!
All your oranges!

At other times, as with some history-literacy hour links, the mathematics calculation may also be an integral part of an historical investigation. This is particularly relevant to making time-line calculations in order to consider sequence, duration and causes and effects. Numerical calculations are also fundamental in organising and making probabilistic interpretations of data: for example making inferences about reasons for changes in population size, occupations, movement, family size in your locality, and the extent to which they reflect national changes (NNS 6: 113–17). Children could devise techniques to analyse the proportions of Palladian buildings in photographs to see how accurately they reflect the 1:1.6. proportions of the Golden Rectangle (described on page 66) in order to demonstrate the influence of Greek architecture on

written by Edward and mike
. pictures by Edward and mike

"Oranges oranges get your oranges!"

"Oranges oranges roll up oranges"

"5p for1, 10 p for 2, 15p for 3, 20p for 4, 25 for

"all your orages"!

Figure 5.4 Mike's and Edward's street cries written in a literacy hour could equally well have been part of a numeracy hour

subsequent buildings. *A Teacher's Guide to Maths and the Historic Environment* (English Heritage 1998b) is packed with further ideas, and museums such as the Weald and Downland Open Air Museum are developing structured numeracy programmes linked to museum visits.

The examples given in Chapter 3 of opportunities to develop mathematics concepts through historical enquiries remain appropriate (NNS 1: 40). They have been linked to the key objectives of the numeracy framework from Reception to Year 6 (Table 5.2). The numeracy strategy explicitly states that 'you need to look for opportunities for drawing mathematics experience out of a wide range of children's activities. Mathematics contributes to many subjects of the curriculum,

Table 5.2 Opportunities within the National Numeracy Framework for developing skills and understanding in mathematics through historical enquiries

	R	Y1	Y2	Y3	Y4	Y5	Y6
Numbers and the number system Calculations and Problem Solving	Recognise number names, order in familiar contexts, count 1-10, e.g. birthdays – cards, badges. I am ☺. My sister is ☺.	Count to 20; count on and back from any small number, e.g. personal time line calculations.	Count, read, write, order whole numbers to 100: count on; back, calculations using appropriate operations, e.g. Time-line calculations over 100 years.	Read, write, order count on, back, numbers to at least 1000, e.g. 1000 year time-line. Calculations within and between periods. Units of time and relationship between them. Calculations involving days, weeks, months, years, e.g. diaries, journeys, newspapers, timetables.		Use 4 number operations to solve word problems involving numbers, quantities, including time, e.g. map calculations, change in populations, land use; time-line calculations.	Use appropriate operations to solve word problems involving numbers and quantities, e.g. rations, ships supplies, manufacture and trade figures.
Measures		Compare 2 lengths, masses, capacities by direct comparison, measure using uniform non-standard units: compare old and new artefacts: e.g. cooking utensils, farm tools, irons, e.g. length of old building.	Estimate, measure, compare, lengths, masses, capacities, using suitable standard measures, e.g. length: museum artefacts, buildings, mass, capacity; old recipes.		Know and use relationships between familiar units of length, mass, capacity. Use appropriate number operations to solve problems, e.g. old recipes, diet, loads carried.	Understand area measured in square centimetres. Model making: Tudor houses, Greek church.	
Shape and Space		Shapes of doors, windows, towers in old building: tiles, bricks.	Shapes in buildings; tiles, slates. Use mathematical vocabulary to describe position, dissection, movement e.g. maps, journeys.				Read coordinates in all 4 quadrants (maps, journeys).
Data handling				Organise and interpret numerical data in simple lists, tables, graphs e.g. census returns, street directions, graveyard studies, parish records, trade figures, questionnaires and surveys.			Solve a problem by extracting and interpreting information presented in tables, graphs, charts.

often in practical ways' (NNS 1: 16). It identifies opportunities to collect data, by counting and measuring of all kinds, to relate ratio, scale, position, direction and coordinates to maps, to relate problems to the measurement of time, in days, weeks, years, decades, centuries. The National Curriculum also identifies opportunities to make these links. With imagination they can be developed both within the numeracy hour and extend beyond it. Historical questions can be identified and data collected from a site visit: measurements, gravestone information, shapes and patterns in buildings and fabrics. Key knowledge and skills in mathematics can be developed through teaching and activities in the numeracy hour, and linked to work in other subjects in the plenary session (NNS 1: 14); founded on sound understanding of the skills required, investigations can extend well beyond the numeracy hour, if they are interesting, and enhance relevance and coherence in a creative curriculum.

History and the numeracy hour: two examples

Besides applying mathematical calculations to historical enquiries children can gain historical insights by finding out how people in the past represented numbers and worked out arithmetic. Robin Foster, a colleague who lectures in primary mathematics education, made this point when I discussed this section of the book with him. 'The arithmetic we take for granted as simple or trivial taxed great minds in the past', he explained. 'Making children aware of how mathematics developed, and how others too found it difficult can be supportive and illuminating.' It was not long before he was persuaded to put his theory into practice. Here are his plans for two numeracy hours he taught to a Year 2 and a Year 6 class.

Year 2, tens and units in a Victorian classroom
Resources:
Picture of a Victorian school room (e.g. Robson 1874)
Picture of a Victorian abacus, Robson 1874 (Figure 5.5)
A modern two-pronged abacus
Worksheets with empty two-pronged abaci for children to complete

Desired Learning Outcomes
At the end of the session the children will have

- used vocabulary relating to the passing of time; identified similarities and differences between their classroom and a Victorian classroom using visual sources (H. 1b, 2b, 4a, 6b/c)
- have seen ways of representing tens and units and relate this to particular numbers

Mental Activity

Have a piece of wire or string with six beads on it. Show the children the beads. *How many beads are there?*

Separate and cover up some of the beads with your hand. How many are hidden? *How many can you see?*

Repeat this for other values of beads. Talk about how in earlier days children did not have much equipment to help them with their mathematics.

Main Session

• Show the children the picture of the Victorian classroom

The picture is in black and white, is it a photograph? Imagine the scene in colour. How is it different from our classroom? How is it the same? What do you think the object in the picture is for? What is an abacus?

• Show the children the close up picture of the Victorian abacus

How could you count using this? What happens if I wanted to show 23? Demonstrate how you could have 23 beads or use 20 (as two tens) and three as three ones. Show a simplified idea of using a two-pronged abacus to show numbers up to 99.

Figure 5.5 A Victorian abacus (Robson 1874)

• Individual or group work

Supply the children with pictures of two-pronged abaci and ask them to represent particular numbers. (Vary the numbers according to the individuals.) Use the abacus to show 56. If you had five beads, what number could you make? Which is the biggest/smallest?

• Plenary

Relate their answers to the Victorian abacus. Allow them to compare their results. *What about numbers which are greater than 99?*

Figure 5.6 Place value using a Victorian method

Year 6, Elizabethan multiplication

Gelosia algorithm – background information

This method, which was used in the reign of Queen Elizabeth I to multiply two-digit numbers, was probably introduced from India. The example shows how it is used to multiply 13 by 49 (Figure 5.7).

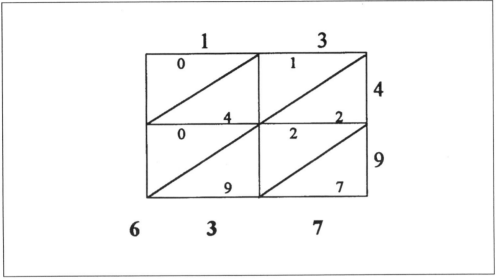

Figure 5.7 Example showing the working of Gelosia algorithm

- Draw a lattice grid of 2 x 2 cells; divide each cell with a diagonal line as shown.
- Put the numbers to be multiplied above and to the right.
- Multiply each digit on the top by each digit on the right; record the tens part of the number at the top left of the cell and the units in the bottom right of the cell.
  1 x 4 = 04
  3 x 4 = 12
  3 x 9 = 27
  1 x 9 = 09
- Add the digits diagonally starting from the bottom right to obtain the final multiplication result of 13 x 49 = 637.

Careful consideration of the place value will reveal that the only units in the result are in the bottom right-hand part of the grid. The next three digits above and to the left are the tens digits, the next diagonal represents the hundred digits and so on. This is an indication of how the algorithm works, but is not really a requirement of anyone successfully employing it.

Year 6, Numeracy hour: Designing and working some 'Tudor' calculations

Resources:

Worksheets with empty Gelosia grids

Desired Learning Outcomes

Children will:

- have considered possible multiplication problems people in Elizabethan times may have needed to solve; that they used a calculation method different from those taught today which was probably introduced from India (H H2a, b);
- be able to compute these problems using an Elizabethan method (Gelosia).

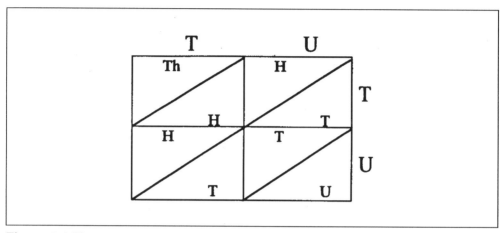

Figure 5.8 Place value demonstrated in Gelosia algorithm

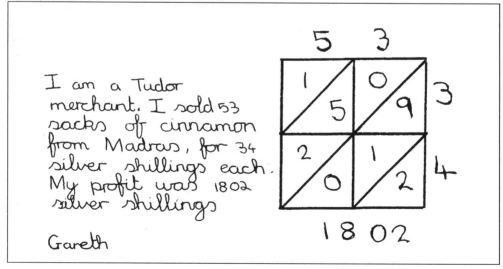

Figure 5.9 'Elizabethan problem' calculated by Gelosia algorithm

Mental Activity
Oral multiplication questions (e.g. 7 x 3)
Teacher records answers on board using lattice type grid

Main Session
Brainstorm possible two-digit multiplication problems people in Elizabethan times might have needed to calculate (e.g. English pirates capture Spanish mule train of 52 donkeys in central America, each carrying 25 bags of silver coins; profit from 30 sacks of peppercorns from Madagascar sold at 63 shillings a sack; 1 quart of beer per day for a ships' crew of 45 on a 30-day voyage; distance of a 25-day voyage, average speed 25 knots each day).

List problems on flip-chart
Demonstrate how to use the Gelosia method to calculate answers to some of the problems. Supply children with blank grids. Ask individuals or groups to work out remaining problems (or design others) using Gelosia algorithm.

Plenary
Individuals demonstrate particular examples.
Compare results and lattices for 37 x 25 and 25 x 37. *Are the results the same? Look carefully at the tens place of the answer. How was it worked out?*
Discuss the place value aspects of this method of recording.

History and Information and Communications Technology

The programmes of study for ICT across the curriculum

Children are required to use information technology sources to support and develop their enquiries in history, to select and analyse information, to share ideas as part of this process, and to organise and communicate their findings (DfEE 1999b). At Key Stage 1 they might gather information (text, images, sound) from a range of sources (CD Roms, videos, television), use and create databases; at Key Stage 2 these sources might be extended to include the Internet, with more emphasis on selecting suitable sources, and working with others to interpret, analyse and check relevance.

This investigative process may be developed at Key Stage 1 by planning and writing instructions, exploring real or imaginary situations through simulations; at Key Stage 2 there may be more emphasis on bringing together and cross-referencing text, images, sound or tables and on reviewing ideas in the light of what others have done.

The findings of the investigation might be presented as a display at Key Stage 1; and at Key Stage 2, through writing brochures, posters, animations or Internet publication on the school website, with a sense of appropriate audiences – other pupils, parents, a wider and impersonal audience. All of these are generic requirements taken from the programmes of study for ICT.

ICT and history: decisions

The programmes of study for history at Key Stages 1 and 2 suggest that the most appropriate ways to use ICT are as sources of information and to make it easier to organise and communicate findings, but clearly this can involve all the other key elements of historical thinking: knowledge and understanding, chronology and interpretations of the past. The wealth of opportunities to use ICT to develop children's historical understanding is daunting and clear decisions need to be made about how this is planned and organised.

Resources referred to in this chapter are listed on page 195.

Using sources

How will the use of ICT support and develop the thinking processes which lie at the heart of historical thinking? How will the sources selected from CD Roms and the overwhelming number of Internet websites be used to encourage children to make deductions and inferences related to their enquiry using the Victorian Web or the Viking Network Web, or the London Blitz, for example. It is possible to access vast quantities of information from all over the world about archaeological sites, about maps, to access the complete collections of art galleries, of museums, statistical archives, newspapers and document archives. But who is going to make the selection? How is children's time going to be managed so that it is not wasted in browsing and reading and copying inappropriate textual information? It may be best for the teacher to preselect sources. This would give teachers (and children) more opportunities for creativity, ownership, considering fitness for purpose and responding to children's interests and locality than the previous dependence on published resources. Sources from distant times and places are immediately accessible. Harrappa (History of South Asia for example) has a good section on the Indus Valley, including a slide tour with script and information. It may be that these are printed out for specific enquiries away from the computer, or that details of an image of a map, artefact or painting are selected and enlarged for use by different groups. However the activities are designed the emphasis must be on asking questions, making deductions and inferences, developing and justifying points of view, related to a larger enquiry and pitched at appropriate levels.

There is also the question of how free pupils should be to find out what we do not want them to! The QCA (2000) Unit 20 on John Lennon advises that 'some of the sites would not be entirely suitable for children to access independently because of the nature of some of Lennon's activities' – and that preceded the allegations that he gave financial support to the IRA and the Workers' Revolutionary Party. 'Maybe your children's enquiries are not as free as you think' as one Hungarian parent put it. Some excellent models for developing historical enquiries using ICT are given in 'Making the Most of ICT at Key Stage 2' (Norton 1999) and 'Any place for a database in the teaching and learning of history at Key Stage 1?' by Smart (1999).

Some websites suggest activities, further enquiries and suggestions for involving parents and other adults. This is a useful strategy for linking home and school work, in ways that could involve parents and the wider community, and break down home–school boundaries. The Public Records Office Learning Curve Gallery, for example, suggests questions to investigate through close scrutiny of images: images to find, describe, categorise as similarities and differences, and further references to explore: 'Was there much difference between rich and poor in Tudor England?' is one example. This is a good model which teachers may wish to adapt for other sites and for their class of children.

Developing investigations

Clearly the teacher also has a management role in supporting and extending an investigation through a sequence of activities identified in the medum-term plan and in preparing classroom organisation to maximise existing resources, by allowing children to plan and develop computer work while away from the computer. Working together to construct and interrogate a database and discuss and interpret findings is one example of planning over time and organising limited resources.

Databases

A database involves collecting information (records), with shared characteristics (fields), in order to look for patterns and trends. These can be recorded graphically as pie or bar charts, graphs or Venn diagrams. In the context of an historical investigation, such sources may be:

1. street directories, census and parish records of births, deaths, age, sex, occupation, address;
2. other statistics relating to population (illness, height, diet);
3. trade figures (cattle sold at Smithfield, price, weight, numbers);
4. information about buildings or archaeological sites with some shared characteristics (e.g. plans of Roman villas, recording shape, size, hypercausts, mosaic pavements);
5. place-name endings in an area indicating time and date of settlement (Roman, Viking, Saxon).

Such sources could be investigated through asking questions about change and about the causes and effects of change and interpreting the findings in the light of incomplete evidence, uncertainty, probability and what is known of the period. Each child can collect information for at least one record – a gravestone, for example – as part of a churchyard study, complete a 'record sheet' on paper, categorising the information in fields to ensure that s/he can structure the information in this way, then type the record onto the database. Next, when all the information has been collected, each child can fill in a second sheet setting out a question and the correct format for asking this question of the database. When children have the responses to their questions they can fill in the last part of the sheet, saying what inferences they can make from them. This tried and tested method ensures that everyone understands how to use the database, and has equal access to creating and interrogating it in a short time, although the complexity of the questions and sophistication of the deductions can vary considerably. Alternatively children could interrogate an existing database, each constructing a question, finding the information, then trying to interpret it. One interesting finding from a local workhouse database was that most of the inmates were described as paupers; one of the few other groups was 'female school teachers'. Deductions? Another finding was that there were few girls in the workhouse but a lot of young boys. Reasons?

Simulations and interpretations

The Internet, CD Roms, television and video offer enormous opportunities to identify compare and explain different ways in which the past is represented. One Tudor England website for example has not only Tudor portraits, documents, maps, buildings but also links with a database of references to films about the Tudors. But it is the quality of the selection of excerpts focusing on the same person or event, comparison with other sources and the class-led discussion about purposes and validity that will develop children's understanding of interpretations, and enable them to make and evaluate their own through parallel role-play activities.

Developing historical imagination

Websites and CD Roms allow children to 'walk through time', to wander around the 'Forum Romanum', move around inside buildings, for example through Tutankhamun's tomb in the Wonders of Ancient Egypt. They allow children independence within clear constraints to follow their own enquiries based on evidence which could be developed either through role-play, story, or in creating information literature.

Mike Corbishley's and Mick Cooper's CD Roms, Real Romans, Real Victorians, Real Castles (1999), are supported by books which help to make coherent links between work at and away from a computer, which they and others think is desirable. The Aztecs has teaching notes and portable booklets available from the site. Evaluation of history books published to support the 1991 National Curriculum recommended more movement back and forth between text and images.

Historical imagination may also be enhanced through using old films and records of popular songs as sources to trace changes in leisure activities, and in ways of life since the 1930s.

Time-lines

There are also opportunities for children to work in collaborative groups to collect information for time-lines using websites, to cross-refer different aspects of change within and across periods, to discuss causes and effects, to cross-reference changes, consider difference in pace. Spartacus Educational traces themes – for example food – across Greek, Roman, Viking and Tudor times. Activities can involve teachers, parents, neighbours. Text and images can be pasted onto time-lines, rearranged and modified in ways which would previously have been too time-consuming, and again this could be organised to allow individual, group and the whole class to work, over a period of time, on a shared theme. There are lots of opportunities for mathematical time-line calculations here, as demonstrated in the mathematics and games sections of Mark Millimore's Ancient Egypt website and in the BBC History 2000 project which offers multilevel time-lines of the histories of England and Scotland from Neolithic times, with photographs and 3-D online models. One innovative student recently scanned in digital images from her pupils' photographs of themselves from birth to five, and put these on their time-lines so that they could add the captions.

Organising and communicating information

Word-processing can be used to develop historical thinking if it is used, not as a typewriter, but to organise information; for example by moving information around on a writing frame (see page 119); to sort into categories; into arguments for and against; to sequence events, or instructions; to put things in order of significance; to structure a report, an explanation or an argument; to highlight key points.

ICT offers exciting opportunities for communicating the findings of an enquiry: at Key Stage 1 word-processing to make explanatory labels and descriptive captions, picture stories; at Key Stage 2 for desktop publishing posters, information brochures, newsletters, which raise questions, present arguments, recount observations and visits. These can be supported by displays, videos, slides, audio tape. They can be disseminated to a variety of audiences through a school website, and shared through e-mails with partner schools involved in similar investigations, but perhaps in different localities, using text, digital images, databases; to compare changes since the 1930s in a mining village, an agricultural village and a suburb for example. 'For pupils the key asset of ICT is not to access vast amounts of information, but the facility to organise and manage the information with a view to making sense of it' (Haydn 1999: 103).

History, music and information technology

> Compose World Junior is a good example of resources which illustrates the potential for teaching history through IT, within an integrated curriculum.
>
> (Hamel 2000: 6–7)

Activities in music and history are also linked to art and literacy. Materials have so far been produced for Ancient Egypt, the Ancient Greeks and the Aztecs. Websites offer sample activities that can be developed through related software and teacher's notes.

To investigate the question, 'Who Were the Ancient Greeks?' for example, the Ancient Greeks theme pack has four frameworks: The Odyssey in which Greek boys in school learn to play the lyre and recite epic poems; the Battle of Troy; the Phaecian Games (from which the Olympic Games develop) and the Blind Bard Demodecus who recites the *Odyssey*. These frameworks cross-refer so that it is possible to move between them. Within each framework there are suggested starting points for developing enquiries; the Greek school could lead into finding out more about Greek writing, literature or types of Greek scales, music and musical instruments. Such enquiries lead children into an enormous variety of other related websites and involve all the key elements of historical thinking. In the Battle of Troy framework, the statement that 'The Greek soldiers were "Hoplites"' offers a link to a website on Socrates, who was a Hoplite. The Phaecian Games links to the Olympic Games virtual Museum, the Blind Bard to a mythology website showing pictures of the story of competition between Apollo and Marysyas.

There are opportunities for enquiries that involve all the key elements of historical thinking. The Bard's singing about Apollo links to a website offering contrasting interpretations of Apollo, ranging from 490 BC to those of Tintoretto in 1731 and Redon in 1910. Websites related to the Trojan Horse offer different versions of the story, including Tennyson's the Lotus Eaters, images of the Trojan Horse from Ancient Greece to Tiepolo (as well as a wealth of other myths and legends besides). There are endless opportunities to make inferences and deductions about a variety of visual sources: artefacts, buildings, pottery, and of course music. Questions can be raised about authenticity; what might a lyre have sounded like? How do we know? How was it made? There are opportunities for comparisons, across cultures as well as over time: comparisons between Ancient Greek lyres and similar Ethiopian and Egyptian instruments, for example. Specialised vocabulary is explained, illustrated and used: (epsilon and phi) and links with modern usage are explained (gymnopaedia, lyric, hymn). Throughout, suggested activities show how knowledge and understanding can be communicated in exciting ways, through music-making, dance, story, role-play and reconstruction.

These resources offer enormous advantages: websites linked to a central story and suggested enquiries and activities. They are much cheaper than books. They allow children to plan their own enquiries, enquiries can easily be differentiated; teachers can even modify text if appropriate. An enormous variety of historical sources can be immediately accessed and selections made. Images can be manipulated, and printed to support children's individual enquiries, or shown on large screens for class and group work. Most importantly the teacher is free to select, from this cornucopia, to plan enquiries appropriate for particular children and classes. This of course makes exciting creative and intellectual demands on teachers' subject knowledge and pedagogy.

What a long way we have come since the Ancient Greeks case study from the early days of the National Curriculum (pp. 65–78). Yet, this is still relevant. This is also based on tales from the Odyssey, as a starting point for finding out about Greek poetry, music and Greek history. But how much more sophisticated children's understanding can be. Finding out how lyres were made, what they looked like, how they may have sounded, how they have developed across different cultures and been portrayed over time, making Greek music which is surely more complex than the rubber bands and paper tubes in the case study. But, all this sophistication and learning is more dependent than ever on sophisticated teaching.

A case study
As part of their study of Ancient Greece, Thomas's group, in his Year 6 class, were asked to

- find out about music in Ancient Greece from a variety of sources;
- to think about how time and place can influence the way music is created, performed and heard.

They visited the 'music school' on the ESP website, and joined the Greek boys learning the prized skills of reciting poetry and accompanying themselves on the lyre. They listened to musical examples showing how the lyre can be 'tuned in different ways to make songs sound different'. This led to a study of the lyre, through a British Museum reconstruction, accessed through 'the Blind Bard'. Then they retold the story of Apollo and Marysas in their own words as a prelude to composing their own musical competition, choosing instrumental sounds they thought closest to the Greek originals. Finally they then accessed a website containing a variety of images of Apollo, selecting pictures of the musical duet between Apollo and Marysas (Figure 5.10).

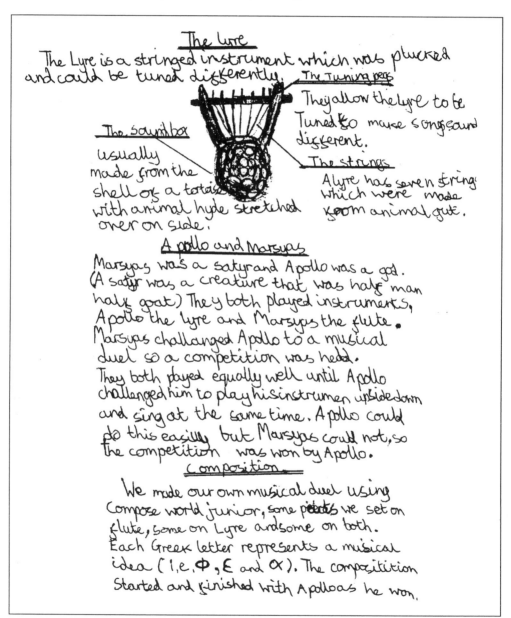

Figure 5.10 The children used the ESP website to reconstruct the musical competition between Apollo and Marsyas

In the following session Thomas's group were asked to identify different ways in which the past is represented and has been subsequently interpreted. They compared three images of the musical duet ranging from 320 BC to AD 1545, discussed the differences between them and possible reasons for them. In the first image there was no tortoiseshell lyre – 'were they hibernating?' In the second, no sound box – 'maybe the artist had never seen a lyre'. By 1545 the lyre has become 'an old violin': Apollo and Marysas, originally depicted as human, evolve into myths and stereotypes. Why? (Figure 5.11).

320bc

This sculpture shows 3 figures, Apollo Marsyas and the Judge. Apollo is wearing a toga, sitting down and listening to Marsyas. Marsyas is bearded and not clothed, he is also not half man half goat.

Apollo's lyre is made of wood and is hollow. The picture is very realistic but there is no tortoise shell. Perhaps they're hibernating.

Marsyas' flute is played like a recorder but it is unclear whether there are two flutes or one with a split handle (If there are two then Marsyas could have won the competition by challenging Apollo to play two lyres which is imposible)

The sculpture is very clear mostly and it is possible that the artist played a lyre.

Rustici

In this coin there is no judge but there are still the figures of Marsyas and Apollo, both are nude. Marsyas apears to have lost and has thrown away his instrument aswell as being tied up. Apollo is younger than Marsyas.

The lyre in this scene has no soundbox so the artist has probably never seen one. Also the flute is not an flute but a set of panpipes

1545

There are 6 people in this scene, 4 observers and two competitors. Apollo is wearing a crown of laurel leaves. This probably came from the tradition of the music competions whose winner would wear a similar crown. Marsyas again is not half man half goat.

The lyre is actually and old violin and he has a bow in his right hand.

The flute in this painting is one long pipe.

Figure 5.11 The children compared three images of the contest between Apollo and Marsyas from 320 BC to AD 1545

Another useful website is The Greeks. This too has interactive activities, an 'Acropolis Experience' and a live web link with the Parthenon.

Chapter 6

The National Curriculum and Action Research

There has been much recent discussion about the nature of research in education and its role in the process of developing practice. Should it be large-scale, statistically reliable studies undertaken by academics and published in esoteric journals, or small case-studies undertaken by practising teachers, drawing from, reflecting on and informing, their professional experience? An example of a large-scale international study of history education is the *Comparative European Study of Historical Communities* (Von Borries and Angvik 1997). Like most large studies it reached broad conclusions; these were not particularly encouraging. History is not taught in primary schools in many European countries and in secondary schools it is usually taught didactically; it does little to challenge or change most pupils' stereotypical thinking and they do not enjoy it. Bodo Von Borries has concluded that what is needed is small-scale, in-depth classroom-based studies. It is to be hoped that current rhetoric about teaching as a research-based profession, increased opportunities for continuing professional development through reflection on practice and partnership between schools and higher education institutions will generate such studies.

The case study described in this chapter was undertaken as a teacher of a class of Year 4 children over two consecutive years (Cooper 1991). It has been encouraging and indeed flattering to observe how, over the last decade, the methodology has become reflected in published materials, and continues to be modified and applied to new contexts. For example Claire Riley (1999), a newly qualified teacher of history in an 11–18 comprehensive school has described how the written evidence test format described in this chapter can be used successfully with pupils from 8 to 18, then describes how she modified it to help a Year 9 class to use a variety of visual and textual sources to explore the big question, 'How healthy were the Victorian towns?' Through evaluating her own practice she goes on to modify and develop the framework further and concludes that good history teaching is systematic literacy work, which can also be closely linked with work in art. This is a good example of the way in which theory, described in Chapter 2, informs research into practice described in this chapter, which is in turn evaluated, modified, developed, and so refines theoretical understandings. This must be the essence of a confident research-based profession in which development is driven by teachers.

The research described in this chapter then is included to encourage busy teachers to consider action research as an in-built part of their approach to developing the 2000 curriculum.

The research design

This investigates the hypothesis that young children can become involved in historical problem-solving, that there is a sequence in the early stages of their thinking which can be evaluated, that teaching strategies are significant in developing children's historical thinking, and that consistent teaching strategies can accelerate this development.

The research was undertaken in two primary schools in an outer suburb of south London. The following extracts of a discussion among eight-year-old children, about the Iron Age chalk horse at Uffington in Berkshire, give an introductory flavour of the study. It is interesting to compare them with the definition of a horse required by Mr Gradgrind in *Hard Times* (Dickens 1854).

'It looks like a bird.'
'It's a horse.'
'They could draw horses.'
'So they had horses.'
'They were hard workers...skilful...artistic...'
'There must be a lot of chalk near the surface.'
'So there wouldn't be trees like oak trees here – not many trees.'
'They could live on the chalk – it's well-drained – the water would run away.'
'The soil would be thin – easy to plough.'
'Whatever tools they used, they must have been able to dig down into the ground to get to the chalk.'
'It must have taken a long time to make – maybe centuries.' They were hard workers...skilful...artistic...'
'They cooperated.'
'They lived in a community.'
'It's not an ordinary horse. It's much different from the ones we see.' 'It must be a special one or they wouldn't go to all that trouble.'
'It's probably a symbol for something – a clue.'

'To bring a good harvest?'

'A symbol of strength?'

'To an enemy? Perhaps the horse brought bad luck so they stayed away.'

'Perhaps if someone was ill they prayed to it. It gave them power when they were ill.'

'Or perhaps they just did it for fun.'

'Maybe they danced around it – or put fires on it and burnt something maybe for the chief's birthday.'

'I don't think they had birthdays.'

'But they had beliefs and ceremonies.'

'Customs.'

These children discuss the geology and the social organisation needed to make the horse, its practical and symbolic significance. They follow through and weigh each other's points. They synthesise them using abstract concepts: cooperate, community, ceremonies, beliefs, customs. They make a distinction between what they know and what they can only speculate about.

Two 'experimental' classes of Year 4 children were taught during consecutive years using carefully defined and documented teaching strategies and compared with a control group in another school taught by an experienced teacher using his own methods. The three groups were initially compared for ability by analyses of variance and covariance using NFER Non-Verbal Reasoning Test BD as covariate. All three groups were taught the same four units of history – the Stone Age, the Iron Age, the Romans and the Saxons – each unit lasting half a term. Each unit was taught within an integrated curriculum with an historical focus. About two hours each week were spent specifically on history.

The teaching strategies for the experimental groups involved discussion of key evidence, differentiating between what you could know 'for certain', what reasonable 'guesses' you could make, and what you 'would like to know' about the evidence. The discussion involved selected key concepts of different levels of abstraction (e.g. arrow, weapon, defence). Each unit of study involved one visit to a local area where there was evidence of settlement at each period and one 'further afield' visit to extend beyond the locality. For example, the Stone Age 'further afield' visit was to Grimes Graves, and the Roman one was to Lullingstone Roman Villa.

At the end of each unit, all three groups took five written 'evidence tests' which each lasted about half-an-hour on consecutive days. In each unit these consisted of five different types of evidence about which children had to make inferences: an artefact (or slide of one), a picture, a diagram, a map and written evidence. The aim was to investigate whether they found 'concrete' evidence more difficult to interpret than more abstract maps and written evidence. A list of evidence used is given in Table 6.1.

Table 6.1 Evidence used in written and oral evidence tests

Unit	Test 1 Artefact	Test 2 Picture	Test 3 Diagram	Test 4 Map	Test 5 Writing
1	Slide. Palaeolithic flint hard axes c. 200,000BC Museum of London. Slide OL91	Slide. Font de Gaume Lascaux. Ray Delvert S. Lot.	Stone circle. The Druids Circle. Caernarvon. Stone circles of the British Isles. A. Burle	Map showing site of neolithic artefacts on North Downs	Petroglyphics from 'How Writing Began' Macdonald
2	Bronze helmet (1BC) Slide BM	Uffington Horse photos	Little Woodbury, Iron Age House plan Wilts. In Cunliffe, R.K. 1974	Lynchets of Iron Age Fields Butser Hill, Hants.	Strabo 1.4.2. Description of British exports
3	Shield boss found in River Tyne. Slide BM.	Detail from frieze of great dish, Mildenhall Slide BM PRB 47	Villa plan Chedworth, Gloucs.	Roman roads across South Downs	Tacitus Annales XII 31-40 Boudicca Revolt
4	Replica of Sceptre. Sutton Hoo ship burial. BM Slide MZ 18	Illuminated manuscript of Harvest made by BM F21985	Plan Saxon church Cirencester	Saxon settlements in Surrey	Beowulf slays Grendel Penguin 1973 trans 824-838

The experimental groups were also given an oral 'evidence test'. The children made a tape-recording of a discussion of each piece of evidence in small groups. During the first year the discussions were led by the teacher, and during the following year, no adult was present.

In addition, the second experimental group was given a story-writing test. They were given a piece of evidence related to the topic which was concerned with religion, beliefs, myth and ritual, so that it invited the children to piece together their knowledge into a coherent picture of the past and to attempt to consider and explain the beliefs and ideas of the period.

An assessment scheme on a ten-point scale was devised for the evidence tests. This was constructed from patterns in the development of deductive reasoning defined in cognitive psychology and in previous research relating this to history. It is not possible to quote it in detail, but it ranges from:

level 1 – illogical;
level 2 – incipient logic not clearly expressed;
level 3 – restatement of information given;
levels 4 and 5 – one or two statements going beyond the information given;
level 6 – an attempted sequential statement inadequately expressed;
levels 7 and 8 – one or two logical sequential statements, where the second statement is based on the first, connected by 'therefore' or 'because';
levels 9 and 10 – a synopsis of previous points, using an abstract concept.

For example, given a map of an area of the North Downs where Stone Age implements have been found, a typical level 3 answer is 'There are clay areas, and chalk areas and steep slopes' (which are given on the map). A level 4 statement is 'They had rivers to get water from'. An example of a level 8 statement is 'Chalky ground is not wet, therefore the tools are found there because Stone Age people could live there. And they were near a river, so they could get water to drink'. An example of a level 10 statement refers to a diagram of an Iron Age hut: 'They had huts. Therefore they could build huts. They had vegetation. Therefore they had materials to make huts. They had houses, shelter and stores'.

A system was devised for analysing group discussions and recording points made using this scale by dividing a page horizontally into ten sections, recording synopses of points under levels and mapping the children's development of each other's arguments (Figure 6.2 p. 151). This analysis could then be transferred to a variety of other diagrammatic forms (Figures 6.3 (p. 154) and 6.8 (p. 163)).

The story-writing test was assessed using a scale based on Ashby and Lee (1987) and Piaget (1932). This ranged from no awareness of ideas, beliefs and values and so no attempt to explain them, through intermediate levels when children mention symbolic artefacts in passing, but do not reflect on the ideas they may represent, and finally to an attempt to suggest the significance of symbols.

The findings

The relationship between interpreting evidence and the development of historical imagination and empathy – implications for story-writing

In analysing the written 'evidence tests' unit 1, The Stone Age, it became apparent that the deductive reasoning scale reflected levels of reasoning, but did not reflect a difference in the quality of the inferences of the control and experimental groups. The experimental groups' answers were more varied and more closely derived from the evidence, while the control group often simply repeated given information which was not rooted in the evidence. The control group displayed more anachronisms and stereotypes, and the assumption that people in the past were simple. Given a plan of a stone circle, for example, the experimental children suggested a variety of possible purposes (KM 'reconed it was for war dances, trading flint, praying'), and they suggested how it may have been made. The control group answers were dominated by repeating received information about 'magic oak trees', 'Druids in white cloaks', and 'scarey magic'.

This difference in quality was examined further in unit 2. Answers were grouped under Collingwood's (1939) three categories of historical enquiry: How was it made? How was it used? What did it mean to people at the time? The following analysis of the experimental groups' responses to the 'Waterloo Helmet' evidence (British Museum slide) shows how they considered each of these questions (although they had not been explicitly asked to do so). They had been asked 'what do you know for certain? What reasonable guesses can you make, and what would you like to know?' Their answers suggest that it is through asking questions of evidence that children gradually learn to consider and attempt to explain the viewpoints of people who lived in other times. It also seems likely that the experimental groups were better able to do this because they had been taught through discursive teaching strategies which encouraged them to make a range of valid suppositions about evidence.

Experimental groups

Written test	*Discussion tapes*
I *How was it made?*	I *How was it made?*
HC Exp 1. Qu I NVR 97	JH Exp 2. NVR 100
'They had metals…they could make things.'	'They made it carefully with the right kind of metals. Certainly they used a mould and little rivets.'
JG Exp 2. Qu I NVR 120	

'They could smelt iron and bronze...they had a furnace for getting iron out of rock.'

IW Exp 1. Qu I NVR 123
'They had charcoal to separate metal from ore.'

ML Exp 1. Qu 3 NVR 102
'I would like to know if the horns were hollow, because if they are it would be lighter.'

RL Exp 1. Qu I NVR 107
'They must have had good minds to remember things
...They knew how to get to learn.'

MF Exp 2. NVR 129
'They had the right tools to shape the metal.'

NH Exp 1. NVR 105
'They could print patterns on it. They had a habit of putting circles on their working.'

GP Exp 1. NVR 133
'They had weapons – shields and swords too. At the British Museum, I copied a sword with a bronze hilt.'

II What was it used for?
(a) For protection in battle
HG Exp 1. Qu 2 NVR 129
'They wore it to protect their heads...they had fights. They made it...they made weapons. They had wars.'

MF Exp 2. Qu 3 NVR 129
'I would like to know how they got the idea of armour, and why did they fight?'

II What was it used for?
(a) For protection in battle
NH Exp 1. NVR 105
'They invented things. They knew how to smelt metal.'
Exp 1.
'It's got horns. It looks fierce – like an ox that could kill. Like a Stone Age hunter's deer antlers – to hide in the bushes. The pattern could show what side you were on so you didn't kill your own men.'
'They fought for food. If there was a bad winter and cattle died...to steal another tribe's cattle, or to cut another tribe's corn if they didn't have enough.'

(b) As a ceremonial symbol or trophy
KC Exp 2. Qu 2 NVR 111
'It might be made for a chief...he would wear it at ceremonies to look special.'

(b) As a ceremonial symbol or trophy
NH Exp 1. NVR 105
'Maybe the more metal you had it showed how high up you were. They'd start with a bracelet 'til they were all covered in metal then they'd be a chief.'

NH   Exp 1. Qu 2 NVR 105
      'They might have used it at
      chariot races...they might have
      had it as a medal. They might
      have liked beautiful things and
      had it as an ornament.'

Exp 2.
'It may have been awarded for
extreme bravery in battle. Or in a
contest for new warriors. Maybe
they had races and contests, and
the armour was awarded for use in
a battle.'

SH   Exp 1. Qu 2 NVR 104
      'It might have been for a
      goddess.'

Exp 1.
'If they found other things in the
River Thames, they may be
offerings to a water goddess, to
thank her for water to drink.'

(c) A commodity to trade

ES   Exp 1. Qu 3 NVR 129
      'How did the archaeologists come
      to find it, because it would tell me
      if it was made there, or if they
      traded them.'

RL   Exp 1. Qu 3 NVR 107
      'And was there one people in the
      place who made them?...if he
      did he would be rich.'

(c) A commodity to trade

Exp 2.
'They could have traded it for
helmets made in another land. Or
maybe for metal to make more
weapons. Maybe, as we learned in
a lesson, Julius Caesar wrote they
used rods of equal weight, or
coins, to trade. They could have
traded it for bronze or iron –
probably for metal of some kind.'

*III   What did it mean to the people
       who wore it?*

PC   Exp 2. Qu I NVR 114
      'They were not afraid of going into
      battle...they looked fierce...they
      put fierce patterns on them.'

*III   What did it mean to the people
       who wore it?*

Exp 2.
'The patterns make it look sort of
mysterious – they look like
flowers...it might mean something
like "long live our tribe" or "our
tribe is the horse tribe". Or special
orders from their God. Or a magic
helmet to help them in battle. Or
the wearer's name. Or to describe
the wearer – how good he was at
hunting or fighting.'

ML   Exp 1. Qu 2 NVR 102
      'I guess it had a kind of strap.'

KL Exp 1. Qu 3 NVR 107
  'Did they make different shapes and sizes, because it would have to fit ...?

DS Exp l.Qu 3 NVR 88
  'I would like to know what it felt like to put it on. It must have been heavy to handle.'

Exp 2.
'The strips at the side probably had vines or strings attached to hold it on to the wearer...they must have put something on it to make it shine...maybe it was measure for the wearer's head.'

Exp 1.
'It's so heavy they probably took it with them and put it on when they got there.'

When the study was planned, it had seemed that making deductions from evidence and historical imagination were different and discrete aspects of historical thinking, and for this reason, separate evidence and story-writing tests were devised. However, analysis of the evidence tests suggested that historical imagination develops through making valid suppositions about how things were made and used in the past and so considering what they may have meant to people at the time, and that this is the vehicle through which historical empathy may develop. Since historical imagination and historical empathy are defined in innumerable ways, their relationship as defined in this study is given in Figure 6.1.

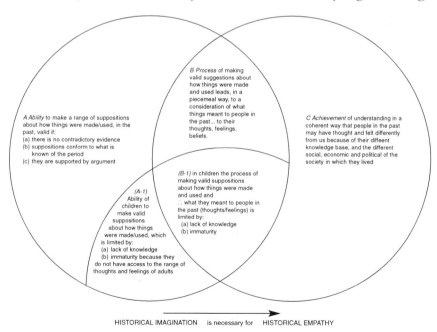

Figure 6.1 Relationship between historical imagination and historical empathy as defined in this study

This has implications for story-writing in history. Analysis of the story-writing tests showed that while children enjoy trying to reconstruct the past through story-writing, and that they do consider and try to explain ideas and beliefs different from their own, their knowledge is limited and they are immature so that they are unable to take a holistic view of society (Furth, 1980). In writing stories, imagination is not necessarily tied closely to evidence, and interpretations of evidence do not have to be argued as they do in discussion. Therefore, anachronisms and misunderstandings are more likely to go unchecked. (Historical fiction is very difficult to write.) In the Stone Age unit, for example, the children were given a postcard of the Barnack Grave, 1800 BC (BM PR 34) with drawings of the grave goods, a walrus or whale-bone pendant, a bronze dagger, a wristguard and a decorated pot, and asked to write a story called 'The Death of the Archer'. About one-third of the children explained this with a story which attached no significance to the grave goods. 'An archer was doing pottery. He might have been shaping it with a dagger. The spear was to protect him. Someone came to the door and threw a flint at him and he fell on the fire.' Others may regard the objects as significant, but they did not reflect on why. Children are caught in a time-warp and see the archer die. 'They bury him with all his things, a bone necklace, a bronze dagger and a large pot,' or the archer was killed in a battle. 'His wife put some of his things around the fire before they burned him.'

At the highest level of response to emerge, stories contained more detailed description of artefacts and more complicated narrative: 'In a village there lived a boy called Balloo. He was learning to do archery. Every three weeks he would get a feather. One day he was given a brilliant surprise – a wristguard; the chance to be a hunter with all the others'. However there was no attempt to explain the significance of the grave goods or the ideas they represented.

It is not suggested that children should never be asked to write stories about the past, but 'Imagine you were …' should be treated with caution. If they are asked to do this, children need to be shown how to relate a reconstruction to evidence. Sylvester (1989) showed how a seven-year-old can use knowledge based on evidence from a pictorial source to write a story about the bubonic plague and the fire, and how a 12-year-old can use directories, plans and logs to write about a day in the life of a Victorian boy. Little (1989) gives two examples of story-writing by ten-year-olds about Spain's conquest of the Inca. In one, a different way of life, hierarchy and ceremony are understood and factual information has been translated into a reconstruction, while in the other, knowledge is thrown in without a sense of time or detail.

Assessing levels of argument

The written evidence tests

In the written evidence tests, the children were given an answer paper which they were told to fill in, pretending they were archaeologists reporting on the evidence (the example shows how Andrew filled in his 'archaeologist's' report on the petroglyphics at the end of the Stone Age unit). Answer papers were laid out to encourage the highest levels of response, based on the ten-point scale described on p. 143. They made a distinction between 'knowing', 'guessing', and 'not knowing', and encouraged children to make two statements for each of these categories, to follow each with a sequential argument and to write a 'conclusion'.

However, it was frequently necessary to look for the underlying logic of the thinking processes behind an answer in order to assess the level of thinking. Often this was obscured by poor spelling or handwriting. An answer may span several levels and would then be scored on the basis of the highest scoring statements within the answer and lower levels ignored. The logic of the answer does not always correspond to the divisions on the paper, so that the statements need to be carefully considered.

The oral evidence tests

Figure 6.2 shows how the oral evidence tests were also analysed on the ten-point scale. These synopses refer to the written evidence used in the Iron Age unit (Strabo 1.4.2).

> Most of the island is level and well-wooded, but there are many hilly districts. It produces corn, cattle, gold, silver and iron. They are all exported, together with leather, slaves and good hunting dogs. The Gauls use these dogs, and their own, for war as well.

Figure 6.3 shows how the levels were then mapped, so that they could be transferred to tables to compare levels of argument achieved in individual written answers and in group discussion over the four periods of study.

Making a distinction between 'knowing' and 'supposing'

In the written evidence tests, the children were asked three questions about each piece of evidence: question one, what do you know for certain? question two, what reasonable 'guesses' can you make? question three, what would you like to know? It is interesting that they were able to make these distinctions. Analysis of the unled discussion tapes – where they were not specifically asked to differentiate between knowing, guessing and not knowing – nevertheless show the discussions dominated by probability words (could be, maybe,

Experimental Group 1

NAME _Andrew_   DATE _6.12.85_

UNIT ONE   THE STONE AGES

EVIDENCE   writing

What do you know FOR CERTAIN from this evidence?		Level 9
they communicated	**Therefore** they made signs for communicating	**Conclusion** they needed other people
they draw	**Therefore** They had thing to draw with	

What reasonable GUESSES can you make about it?		Level 8
they may of had spcshelts thing to do writing with	**Therefore**	**Conclusion** they might of had spcsbell hunting signs
I think it had a meaning	**Therefore** It migh of taken them a long time to get the writing	

What would you LIKE TO KNOW about it?		Level 6
What it ment	**Because** then we could make little word	**Conclusion**
had they got to know what the signs ment	**Because** then we could do stone age writing.	

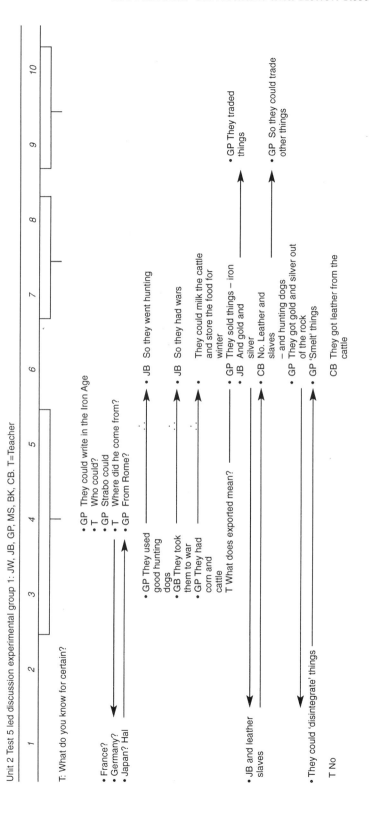

Unit 2 Test 5 led discussion experimental group 1: JW, JB, GP, MS, BK, CB. T=Teacher

Figure 6.2 Synopsis of led and unled discussion showing how it is represented as a diagram

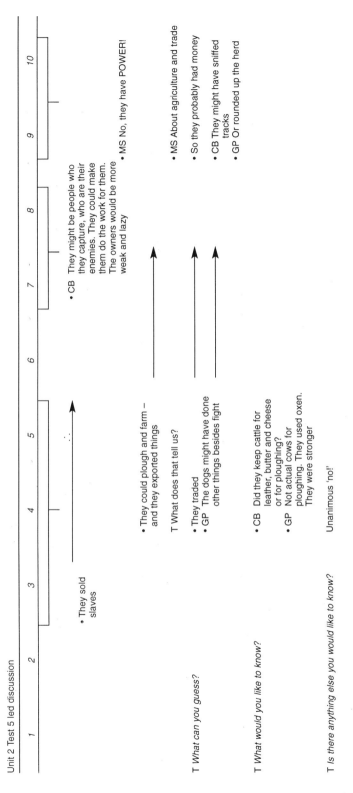

Unit 2 Test 5 led discussion

| | | | | | | | | | |
|1|2|3|4|5|6|7|8|9|10|

• They sold slaves

• CB They might be people who they capture, who are their enemies. They could make them do the work for them. The owners would be more weak and lazy

• MS No, they have POWER!

• They could plough and farm – and they exported things

T *What does that tell us?*

• They traded
• GP The dogs might have done other things besides fight

• MS About agriculture and trade

• So they probably had money

• CB They might have sniffed tracks
• GP Or rounded up the herd

T *What can you guess?*

• CB Did they keep cattle for leather, butter and cheese or for ploughing?
• GP Not actual cows for ploughing. They used oxen. They were stronger

T *What would you like to know?*

Unanimous 'no!'

T *Is there anything else you would like to know?*

Figure 6.2 cont

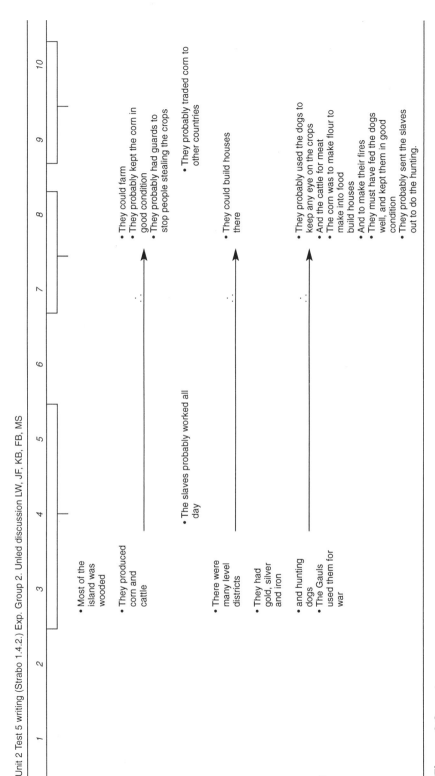

Unit 2 Test 5 writing (Strabo 1.4.2.) Exp. Group 2. Unled discussion LW, JF, KB, FB, MS

Figure 6.2 cont

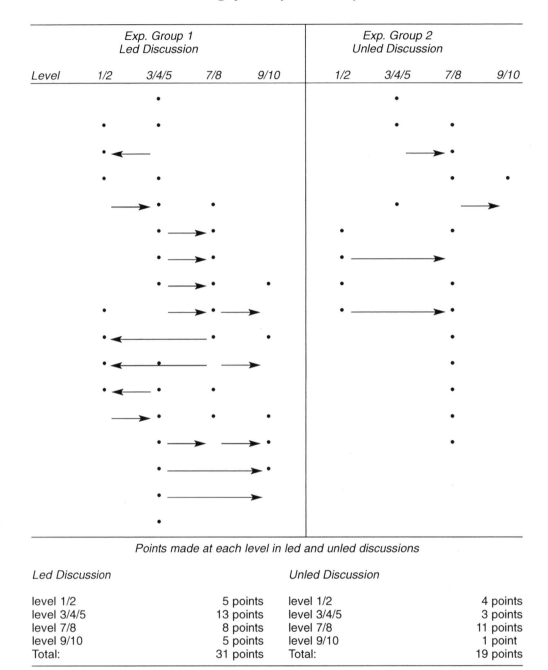

Points made at each level in led and unled discussions

Led Discussion		Unled Discussion	
level 1/2	5 points	level 1/2	4 points
level 3/4/5	13 points	level 3/4/5	3 points
level 7/8	8 points	level 7/8	11 points
level 9/10	5 points	level 9/10	1 point
Total:	31 points	Total:	19 points

Figure 6.3 Led and unled discussions, unit 2, test 5, writing. Strabo 1.4.2

unlikely, I wonder, what you think?). The children occasionally make certainty statements. 'They (the axe-heads) were all chipped and smoothed' and sometimes these are challenged by other children: 'It's got two heads' (cave painting). 'That could be a tail.' 'Bit thick for a tail.'

The unled groups also sometimes mention things that they would like to know. 'It must have been for some reason?' 'How do you think they made the banks?'

It is interesting that in the written evidence tests the children were able to make 'certainty' statements, and reasonable guesses (questions one and two) with almost equal ease. The graph (Figure 6.4) based on analysis of variance tests to compare groups, questions and types of evidence in each unit, shows a significant difference between the types of question, with question three (what would you like to know?) by far the most difficult. The Sheffe test of multiple

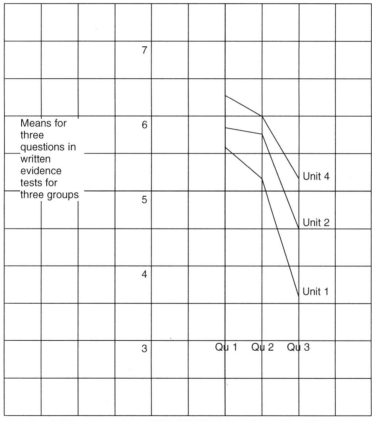

Question 1 What do you know FOR CERTAIN, from this evidence?
Question 2 What REASONABLE GUESSES can you make from this evidence?
Question 3 What WOULD YOU LIKE TO KNOW about this evidence

Figure 6.4 Graph showing means of scores for questions 1, 2 and 3 for units 1, 2 and 4. (Unit 3 was taught and tested but the results were not analysed due to shortage of time)

comparison shows the difference between the first two questions and question three to be significant. These children then are able to make a distinction between knowing and valid suppositions, and they find both types of inference equally easy, but they find it far harder to say what they 'would like to know' about evidence.

Although these results were statistically significant, there were exceptions to the main effects. There were significant interactions between the questions and types of evidence. In unit I, for example, there was little difference in difficulty between knowing and guessing about the cave painting, the plan of the stone circle, or the map. This is not surprising because not much is known about how these things were made or used or what they meant to Stone Age people, even by archaeologists, so there are fertile opportunities for reasonable guesses. On the other hand, it was easier to make certainty statements about axe-heads because these are central to a study of the Stone Age. The experimental groups had three lessons on tools and weapons and had seen them made at Grimes Graves. This is important because it shows how statistically significant main effects are blurred by other variables, by a particular example of a type of evidence, by interest and by motivation.

There do however, seem to be implications for teachers in the general finding that children are equally able to say what they know, and to make reasonable suggestions, but find it difficult to say what they 'would like to know'. It suggests that children of this age do not need to be restricted to repeating 'facts' and that they are able to become actively involved in historical problem-solving. They can learn to control their own thinking, and become increasingly aware of what constitutes a valid supposition. This is an important staging post on the way to true historical understanding. However, 'what would you like to know?' is a question with an unknown starting point, and is too open. It does not encourage children to control their own investigation. This is significant because children are frequently told to 'find out about ...', particularly at the ends of chapters in history books, assuming this encourages motivation and independent learning. These tests suggest that such a question is too unstructured.

Different types of evidence

The study set out to investigate whether children find it easier to make deductions about artefacts and pictures than about more abstract evidence, diagrams, maps and written sources. The relationship between groups, questions and evidence in each unit was statistically analysed using analyses of variance. The findings are shown in Figure 6.5.

Although in unit 1 there was a significant difference between the levels of response to the five types of evidence, and the children found the diagram and the map the most difficult, it is interesting that by unit 2, and again in unit 4, there was no significant difference in their ability to interpret 'concrete' and 'abstract' evidence. This is not to suggest that it is not very important for children to be introduced to artefacts and pictures (which are, at the very least, stimulating sources), but rather that if they are given more abstract evidence as well, as part of a continuum, and have learned to discuss evidence, they can interpret abstract sources equally well. This seems to be because, having learned how to discuss evidence and the kinds of responses required, they can relate abstract evidence to 'concrete' evidence – maybe through visits to sites or museums. The experimental groups had visited Grimes Graves, the British Museum and local sites, and related these to maps, geology, vegetation and relief. They could therefore draw on these experiences in interpreting, for example, the Stone Age axe-heads, the Waterloo Helmet, the plans of the stone circle, the Iron Age hut, and the maps.

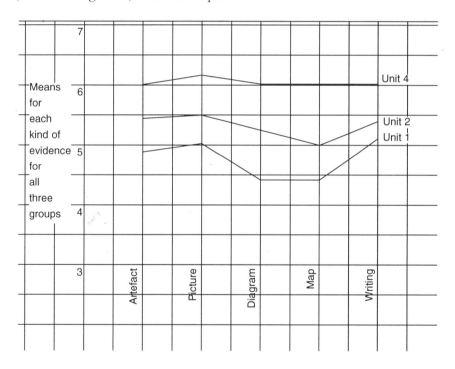

Figure 6.5 Graph showing means of scores for questions 1, 2 and 3 for units 1, 2 and 4. (Unit 3 was taught and tested but the results were not analysed due to shortage of time.) The marking scale is outline on p.143

Their level of response depends, not on the level of abstraction of the evidence, but on language, on concepts and on argument, because remains of the past are only evidence to the extent that they can tell us about the people who made and used them. Children need to experience physical evidence, and to learn to discuss it, if it is to have meaning for them. They are then able to transfer this process to new evidence, and to more abstract evidence.

There are implications here for older students. It has often been assumed that artefacts and pictures are more appropriate for younger children who cannot read and write easily. However, if tangible sources are not easier to interpret, this strengthens the case for using a range of sources at any level of study.

Again, it is important to bear in mind that while the main effects shown in Figure 6.5 are statistically significant, there were variations in this pattern, influenced by particular examples of evidence, and by teaching strategies. In unit 4, the level main effect across the five kinds of evidence resulted from opposite trends across the experimental and control groups, although the span was only across one mark. It is likely that the control group found the Beowulf extract easier to interpret than the other evidence because they had more experience of 'comprehension exercises', but they had not learned how to interpret historical evidence.

Using learned concepts

The concepts which children had been taught in each unit as 'spellings' and which they had learned to use in discussing key evidence during class lessons the following week were used spontaneously by at least some of the children in both the written tests and the taped discussions. It was also encouraging that in unit 4, they were using vocabulary which they had learned in connection with previous units, transferring it to a new period and new material. Not surprisingly, the children in the control group who had not learned specific concepts only used those which were labelled in the evidence, and these were rarely abstract concepts. Figure 6.6 and Figure 6.7 show how children used concepts they had learned in previous units in both written and oral evidence tests.

Although no claim is made that the children totally understood the abstract concepts they used (e.g. vegetation, belief, power, agriculture, transport, society, religion), it seems that these concepts are becoming part of their own vocabulary.

It may be that the experimental groups were able to make a far greater range of valid suppositions about the evidence because they had a conceptual framework of both concrete and abstract concepts to which they could relate new pieces of evidence, even if the concepts themselves were not mentioned in their answers. Freedman and Loftus (1971) concluded that concepts play an important part in organising semantic memory. For example, in interpreting the written evidence in the Iron Age unit (see p. 149) many children make deductions concerned with trade, agriculture, metal production and social structure.

IW 'We know that Grece people traded with us...they must have had something to trade with.'

FF 'We know that gold, silver and iron are all exported across the sea.'

NH 'They had corn and cattle...they could farm and so they had learned to live in one place.'

MF guessed that 'since they had gold, silver and iron, they had miners' and he wondered how they mined and transported it because he had seen neither mining tools nor Iron Age boats in pictures.

Similarly, in interpreting the illuminated Saxon manuscript showing harvest, children in the experimental groups focused on ideas connected with agriculture, community, and communication. They discussed crops, farming methods and the cycle of the farming year.

RD 'The people seem to be cutting logs and transporting them maybe to trade them – if they lived near a forest.'

They refer to the jobs people are doing and the relationship between them, and make various suggestions about the meaning of the writing.

It seems then that not only do children enjoy learning to use and spell 'hard words', but that learning key concepts gives them a reference point, or framework, to apply to new material, and that this helps to generate a range of new ideas about it.

Led and unled group discussion

The content of the discussion was similar in both the led and unled groups. It was concerned with how the evidence may have been used and what it may have meant to those who created it, although the children had not been asked at any point to consider these aspects. However, the groups differed in the way they expressed their ideas. The led groups tended to make general statements and seemed to assume that the teacher knew where the discussion was leading, whereas the unled groups paid more attention to physical description, and sometimes explained their ideas through valid stories and images, about brave warriors for example, who may be commemorated by a stone circle, or who may have hidden their treasure there and defended it. However, in both the led and unled groups, there was genuine argument. They both made some illogical points. In the unled groups, they were either ignored or corrected, with respect, by another child. In the led groups, it was usually the teacher who queried them. In both groups, the children developed each other's points and the quality of the discussion improved over the four units. There was an increase in the

1 cm represents the use of the concept in one evidence test on one or more occasions

■ represents led discussion groups (Exp 1)
▨ represents unled discussion groups (Exp 2)

Led (Exp 1)		*Unled* (Exp 2)	
Concrete	11	Concrete	9
Abstract	9	Abstract	8
Superordinate	10	Superordinate	1

This bar chart shows how both the led and unled groups used their taught vocabulary in unit 2 discussions and, when appropriate, used concepts learned in unit 1. The led groups, however, used more superordinates than the unled groups

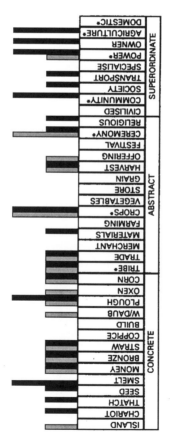

Note: * concepts learned in unit 1.

Figure 6.6 The taught concepts in unit 2 used in discussion tapes

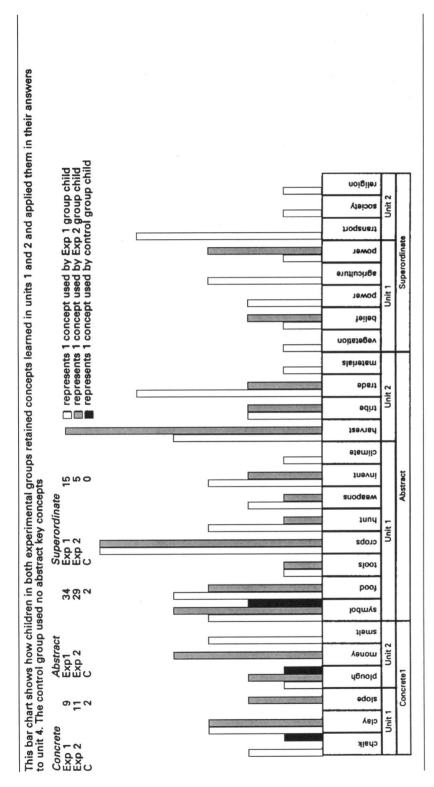

This bar chart shows how children in both experimental groups retained concepts learned in units 1 and 2 and applied them in their answers to unit 4. The control group used no abstract key concepts

	Concrete	*Abstract*	*Superordinate*
Exp 1	9	34	15
Exp 2	11	29	5
C	2	2	0

□ represents 1 concept used by Exp 1 group child
▨ represents 1 concept used by Exp 2 group child
■ represents 1 concept used by control group child

Figure 6.7 Concepts taught in unit 1 or unit 2 which were used in written evidence tests in unit 4 by Exp 1, Exp 2 and control group children

numbers of points made and in the number of sequential arguments, and a decrease in the number of illogical points. The structure of the discussions differed slightly in the led and unled groups. The led groups tended to explore all the possibilities suggested by one point, then move on to the next point whereas the unled groups usually followed up a point with one further argument, then made a fresh point. Sometimes, they backtracked, and ideas were less systematically explored.

It seems then that both led and unled discussions have a place in helping children to interpret evidence. If children have learned the thinking patterns required, discussion in small groups without the teacher may sometimes be more valuable than teacher-led discussion; children are more able to explain their ideas in their own way, to defend them and so to make them their own. This has implications for classroom organisation and for the value of group work not directly led by the teacher (Figure 6.8).

Teaching strategies

Visits

The children were able to transfer information learned on visiting a site to new evidence. For example, on the visit to Farthing Down, they had been asked how, if they had lived there in Neolithic times, they could have made a dry, warm, comfortable shelter, what they could have eaten, where they might have found water, how they might have made tools, weapons and pots. When given a map of another similar area of the North Downs they were able to apply these points to the new map and make a range of deductions and suggestions in their written answers. Table 6.2 shows the information children had discussed on their visit to Farthing Down on the left. This visit stimulated their deductions about the map of a similar but unknown area which are given on the right.

The scores were surprisingly high for such abstract evidence; this seems to be because the visit enabled the children to relate real experiences and images to the map. As AW wrote in his conclusion 'This is the best evidence game'!

Similarly, in the Iron Age unit, they had again visited Farthing Down to trace the lynchets, the soil banks formed by turning the plough, which indicate Iron Age field patterns. Figure 6.9 shows how they were able to transfer discussion of these to the Iron Age map fields at Butser, on the South Downs.

At the end of unit 2 the children were given a previously unseen map of Iron Age fields on Butser Hill in Hampshire. In their written answers, experimental group 2 developed between them many of the arguments inherent in this evidence, which showed lynchets and trackways.

Table 6.3 analyses how children in the written answers related the new evidence about Butser to their visit to Farthing Down, and also to their class

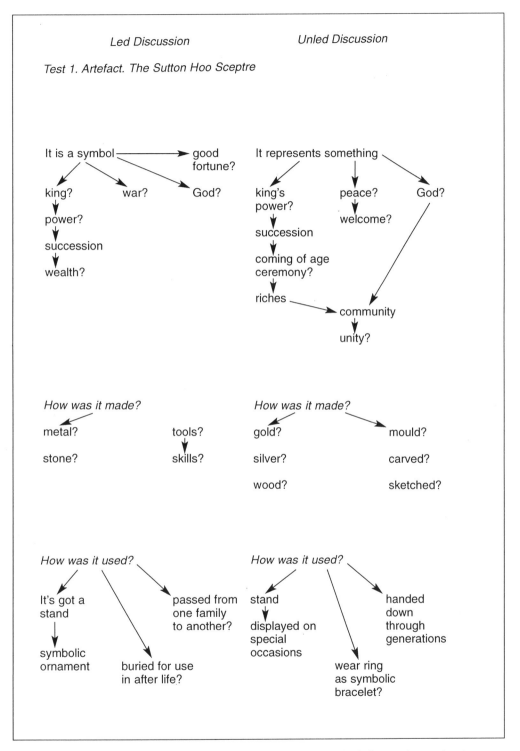

Figure 6.8 A comparison of the content of the led and unled discussions about previously unseen evidence. Unit 4: The Saxons

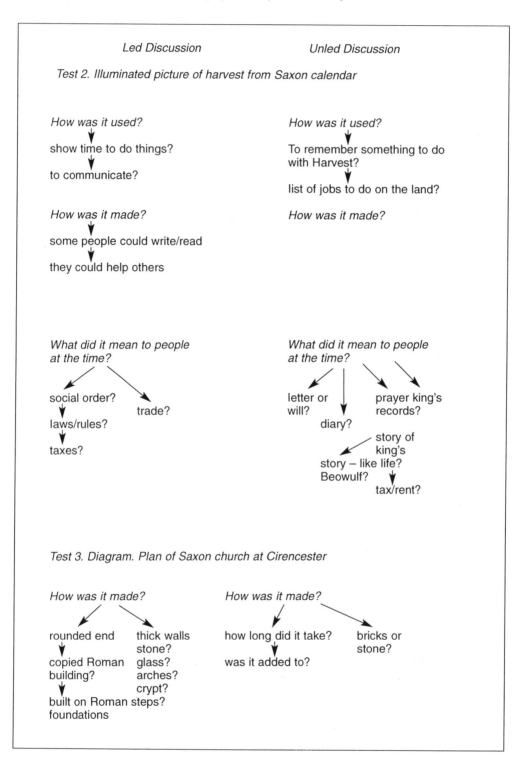

Led Discussion   Unled Discussion

Test 2. Illuminated picture of harvest from Saxon calendar

How was it used?   How was it used?
  ↓   ↓
show time to do things?   To remember something to do
  ↓   with Harvest?
to communicate?   ↓
                                  list of jobs to do on the land?

How was it made?   How was it made?
  ↓
some people could write/read
  ↓
they could help others

What did it mean to people   What did it mean to people
at the time?   at the time?

social order?   letter or   prayer king's
  ↓   trade?   will?   ↓   records?
laws/rules?   diary?
  ↓   story of
taxes?   ↙   king's
                                  story – like life?
                                  Beowulf?   ↓
                                           tax/rent?

Test 3. Diagram. Plan of Saxon church at Cirencester

How was it made?   How was it made?

rounded end   thick walls   how long did it take?   bricks or
  ↓   stone?   ↓   stone?
copied Roman   glass?   was it added to?
building?   arches?
  ↓   crypt?
built on Roman steps?
foundations

Figure 6.8 cont

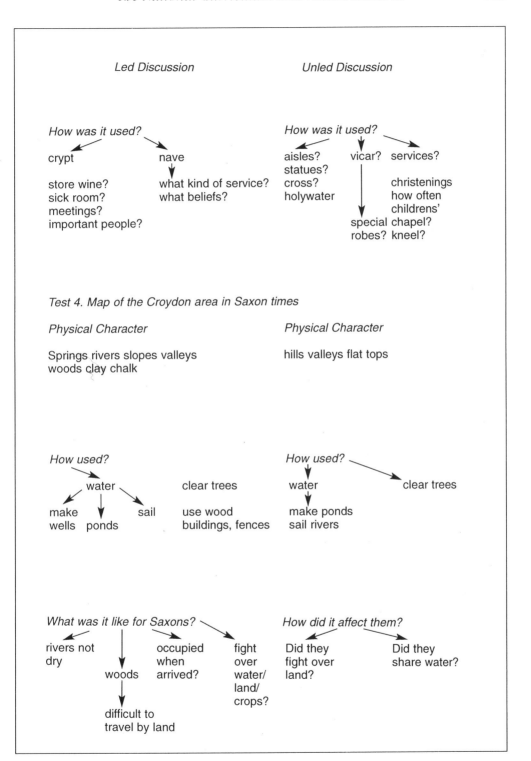

Figure 6.8 cont

Table 6.2 Examples of written answers, showing how visit to Farthing Down helped children to interpret the map

Evidence discussed on visit to Farthing Down	Children's use of this evidence applied to the map (Exp Group A) Written Evidence
Geology: Top of Down is chalk with flints. Sparse vegetation and well-drained.	CL Qu 1. They had a lot of chalk. They could build huts on it because it's flat. They would not build a hut at the bottom of the hill because the water would not run away. (Score level 8) AM Qu 2. They would have camped on the slopes because when it rained the rain would run down the slope, their camp would not be flooded and their huts would not get destroyed. (Score level 7) CL Qu 3. I would like to know what flint implements were used for because they already had hand tools for killing animals. (Score level 6)
Clay soil – sticky – heavy	HC It has got a lot of clay on the surfis...it must of been soggy. It must of been wet. (Score level 7) IW Qu 2.1 can guess that they made things...they would use clay to built pots. We can also guess that there is chalk...there is flint. (Score level 8) HC Qu 2. There might have been a lot of wetness... it could of been cold. There might of been Stone Age people living there...they might of been living on the chalk bits.
In valley bottom there is marsh and a stream	ML Qu 2. They might have routes to the rivers... they would have an easy way to go. They used pots to get water...they can get water in time. (Score level 8)
Hachures show slopes	KM Qu 1. We know that Hachures mean steep slopes...the hachures on the map mean there are shallow and steep slopes. (Score level 7)
Vegetation (+Geology) grass on top yew and oak on clay slopes	JW Qu 2. I can guess what kind of trees grew there...I think oak and fir trees grew there. There were big chalk and clay areas where they could make pots. They could of lived near the clay area so they wouldn't have to walk far. (Score level 8) CL Qu 2. We can guess which plants they used for medicine...some people knew which plants cure illnesses. We can also guess which plants and leaves they used for a bed...they would choose the best things to make it. So they would select things to use. (Score level 7)
Animals	ES Qu 3. I would like to know if animals lived there when Stone Age lived because I want to see if they ate small animals.

Examples. Experimental Group 2. Unit 1. Test 4. Showing use of visit in interpreting map

| *Geology*: chalk/flint, clay, slope, wind, river | PC (level 8) Qu 1. They found that chalk sucks the water through it...we know it was dry. They lived in places like Farthing Down. DF (level 9) Qu 2. They lived near to chalk and clay areas...they didn't have to go far to get flints. They lived near slopes...they were in a place with not many trees. They knew exactly where to live. |

Table 6.2 cont

Evidence discussed on visit to Farthing Down	Children's use of this evidence applied to the map (Exp Group A) Written Evidence
	JG (Level 8) Qu 2. I guess they could have shelter from the cliffs...they would be safe. They would have water...they could have land for farming on the chalk soil.
	FB (level 8) Qu 2. They probably went fishing in the river...they probably had quite a lot of fish. They probably had to wash in the river...they probably didn't wash much!
	JG (level 8) Qu 1. Neolithic people must have been in the area...they had camps there. Trees might be in great numbers on the clay soil...they had shelter.
Vegetation	MF (level 7) Qu 3. Why they chose that place. What animals lived there, because I'd like to know what they ate.
	RF (level 7) Qu 2. I can guess there must have been a lot of woods...I can guess there must have been lots of animals nearby. I know there
Animals	must have been a lot of food nearby.

discussion on Iron Age farming, and finally to their own ideas. This shows how they were able to transfer the experience of the visit and following class discussion to new evidence, and, in so doing, also to form their own valid suggestions and questions.

The visits probably also helped them to discuss the plans of a stone circle, an Iron Age hut, and a Saxon church, although they had not visited similar sites, because they had considered geology, vegetation and relief, and the effects of these on a settlement in each period.

The stimulus of the 'further afield' visit to Grimes Graves and the British Museum probably helped the experimental groups to make a greater range of suppositions than the control group about artefacts, about the Stone-Age axeheads, for example, and the Waterloo Helmet.

Language: discussion, concepts and language as an objective tool

Discussion

Class lessons were based on discussion of selected evidence, using learned concepts. Each unit consisted of four such lessons taught over consecutive weeks. One of the four lessons was based on the local visit to an area of settlement, and one focused on ideas and beliefs.

This study endorsed the importance of learning through open-ended discussion, in which children learn the thinking processes of history. They learn

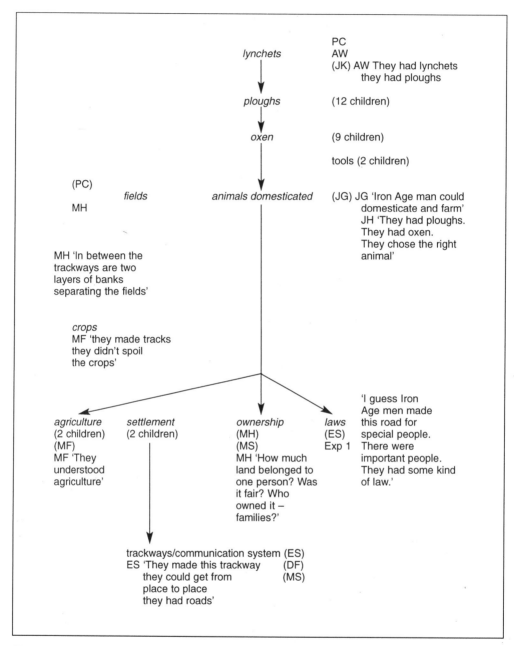

Figure 6.9 How children were able to transfer their discussion of Iron Age field patterns seen on a visit to Farthing Down to a previously unseen map of field systems on Butser Hill, Hants.

Table 6.3 How children, in written answers related new evidence about Butser to their visit to Farthing Down and also to their class discussion about Iron Age farming and finally to their own ideas

Butser Map	Farthing Down Visit	Class Discussion	Own Ideas
PC There are bumps. We know where the fields were	They could use machinery like a plough They farmed They grew crops.	There was probably a settlement there. They probably grew vegetables (re: evidence of beans, vetch, crop rotation)	If they thought a horse was a god or something why did they not use it? (in farming)
JG They had ploughs	They understood how to grow crops. They could farm and domesticate	There might be tools or there might be bones of oxen still there. (re: evidence of bones found, and tools, at Glastonbury) (re: oxen bones similar to modern Dexter)	A cart could carry crops from the field. How long did it take to make (invent?) a cart? If there are bones there, archaeologists could make up an oxen like they make dinosaurs in Natural History Museum
RF I know for certain this map give us clues. I know some people can find these ditches (i.e. I know they exist and what they look like)	I guess they had patterns in soil and chalk (i.e. I know soil or chalk is thin – viz the Uffington Horse)	I guess they had lambs (re: sheep probably Soay, as at Butser) or as JK said 'sheep would give wool and meat and keep the grass down'	
MS They had fields. They must have had a plough	I guess the tracks were for taking the plough across	They might grow things like peas and beans (re: Butser evidence)	I guess the tracks were made of wood. There must have been timber to make them from. I would like to know what transport they had, and we would know what skills they had

Table 6.3 cont

Butser Map	Farthing Down Visit	Class Discussion	Own Ideas
SK They had roads	They could take the oxen across to another field because if the plough went over the corn it would crush it up and it would not grow again	I think had a field of *herbs* (re: discussion of flavouring and preserving)	They could eat them and (use them to) make other foods
MH In between the two trackways are the two layers of banks separating the fields	They must transport the plough through gaps in the banks	The blank bits might be for *settlements* (re: post-hole evidence)	Maybe the owners might live there. Maybe ownership separated by trackways. I would like to know how much land belonged to one person; if they had the same amount and if they lived in families next to each other

that many suggestions are possible, and remain uncertain, and that arguments must be supported and can be contested. This is how criteria for validity become understood. It seems likely that this is the most important factor in the difference between the control group and experimental groups' responses. Firstly, the experimental groups achieved both a higher level of inferential reasoning, and a wider range of valid suppositions. Secondly, the control and experimental groups used the factual information they had in different ways. They were not required to rehearse it in their answers but nevertheless, it underpinned their answers. The control group, however, tended to repeat information given, which was only loosely related to the evidence, and when they went beyond it, they often revealed misconceptions. The experimental groups were more likely to test given knowledge against the evidence. Their suggestions, for example, about the Anglo-Saxon sceptre were dependent on their knowledge of Anglo-Saxon kings and kingdoms, laws and succession.

It seems, then, that discussion is important in the development of historical understanding. However the discussion must be based on selected key evidence. Children need key factual information, but if they learn it through discussion, they do not simply repeat it, but they both retain the information and are able to transfer the pattern of discursive thinking to new evidence.

Concepts

The importance of teaching and using selected concepts of different levels of abstraction to interpret key evidence has already been discussed (p. 158). It was seen that children were able to use abstract, learned concepts as an organising framework against which to test new evidence, even when they did not mention the concept itself. This helped them in discussing the Sutton Hoo sceptre to talk about the king, ceremonies, symbols and laws; Beowulf deductions involved power, vengeance, courage and beliefs. Learned concepts helped children to make a greater range of valid suggestions about evidence, to develop arguments, and so to make suggestions about different attitudes, behaviour and beliefs.

Language as an objective tool

The experimental groups had also discussed the nature of language as a tool for communication. They were able to talk about the relationship between the written and spoken word, the symbolism of language and to suppose how language originated and changed. A child could say of the Stone Age petroglyphics, for instance, 'They made signs for communicating; they had things to draw with; they needed people'. Or 'They wrote strange writing...they had different words from today. This writing is found in Italy...it could have been found in other places'. One child wrote, 'They had to teach each other how to speak...they had to cooperate in making writing'. Another guessed that in different countries they had different signs...if someone went to a different country, he would not understand. It took a long time to carve the signs...they would not move from place to place.

In considering the Strabo excerpt in unit 2, JG wondered 'how long after the Romans the Iron Age wrote'. AW observed that 'they had different language over different times. They did not have the same language everywhere...I would like to know how they made their languages up'.

In unit 4, JG wondered, 'if the Saxons learned writing from the Romans', but AW and DS guessed it was learned through the monks. 'I guess the monks wrote it. It would be in Latin.' 'Monks were taut to read and rit in neat ritting.' SH guessed that since they could write and were good at drawing, 'they probably had lituriture'. In interpreting the extract from Beowulf, children considered the significance of the language. 'I would like to know what Gaet means.' 'I would like to know why Grendel was called Grendel. It sounds strange. Is Grendel a Latin name or an English name?' 'I think that "gable roof" is the bit just below the top of the house.' They also tried to explore the significance of Saxon writing. 'It is a Saxon poem. Therefore they had forms of writing. Beowulf was made up. Therefore it would be a folk tale or a legend.'

Acceleration

The study suggested that if children are taught consistently, applying the same teaching strategies to new material, they learn patterns of thinking that can be transferred, and the quality of their thinking improves. In unit 4, the experimental groups achieved higher levels of deductive argument than in previous units, and used more abstract concepts. It seems then that it is important for children to learn patterns of thinking, and for teachers to be clear what these should be. In unit 4, although the means for all three groups were higher than in the first two units, the means for the experimental groups were much higher than the control group mean (Figure 6.10).

The integrated curriculum

The study did not aim to prove the benefits of learning history through an integrated curriculum. However, the links between responses to the history tests and other areas of the curriculum can be traced. From the science components, the children seem to have learned both to question and respect the technology of other societies.

They discuss how things were made and used. For example, the discussion

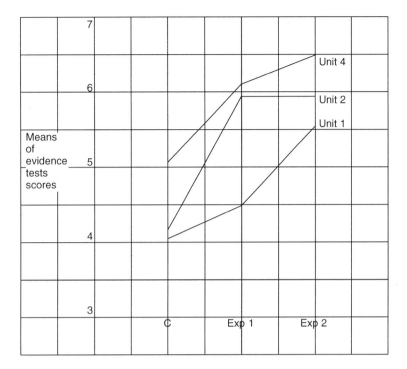

Figure 6.10 Graph showing means of evidence test scores for control and experimental groups for units 1, 2 and 4

of the Waterloo Helmet reflects their knowledge of iron smelting learned in the Iron Age unit. Their experience of historical fiction (e.g. *The Changeling*, Sutcliffe 1974; and *The Bronze Sword*, Treece 1965) may well have helped children to recognise the difference between fact and imagination. There are many examples of children transferring their knowledge of geology, vegetation and relief to maps of other areas; geography probably also influenced their references to trade, transport, and migration of peoples. Art taught the experimental groups careful observation through drawing (slides of cave paintings, Iron Age artefacts in the British Museum, or Anglo-Saxon pottery). It also seems to have taught them both an interest in the techniques and materials used in the past, and an understanding and respect for different interpretations. SH guesses that 'Stone Age people may have kept their oxides in pots and used their hands to paint'. The experimental groups suggest why the Uffington Horse may be unrealistic. DS NVR 88 (Exp 1. Qu 1(7)) owns a horse and brings her own keen interest to bear, in spite of difficulties with spelling!

I kown that they had Horse Because it is a piter of one. They must of copid the Bones of the Horse And the shape of the Horse And it must of bein bukin because of its back legs and the sape of it . . .

MH NVR 135 (Exp 2. Qu 1(9))

> Two of the legs do not join up to the body. Therefore I think that is a special 3D effect. It has whiskers on a kind of chin. Therefore either they have not observed well, or their horse has whiskers.

The dimension of religious education involved the discussion of the symbolism of light and dark in cave painting and in other cultures, the needs and fears of Iron Age people, the nature of Roman gods, the teachings of early Celtic and Roman missionaries. It may be that this helped children to consider reasons for beliefs and rituals in their own and other societies. The mathematics component may have encouraged deductions involving estimates. ('It might take 1,000 people to fill the church. The population must have been big.') They consider shape. One child says of the circle, 'They had another shape in maths', and the Uffington Horse has a 'special 3D effect'. The Iron Age fields are 'square or rectangular'.

A degree of integration, with a clear history focus seems the most economical way, in a crowded curriculum, to allow children to become steeped in a period. It also demonstrates that history involves the history of thought in all disciplines and in all aspects of society, and can, in turn, give a purpose to experiment in science and to calculations in mathematics.

Ways in which teachers can evaluate and develop the National Curriculum in the light of experience and good practice

This research indicates some of the problems involved in assessing patterns in the development of children's thinking in history. However, the study was undertaken as an integral part of class teaching, and refined the thinking of the teacher and the quality of her teaching in the process, so that it suggests that action research by practising teachers is both possible and desirable, and should therefore be supported and encouraged.

It is not necessary for such detailed analysis to be carried out all the time, or by all teachers; the purpose of the study described was to indicate broad patterns of development, and the relationship between different aspects of historical thinking which could form a basis for planning and for on-going assessment by teachers. It is essential that the broad brushstrokes with which the National Curriculum aims to paint a map of the past is also balanced by detailed and carefully focused discussion of key evidence. Young children cannot grasp a holistic view of complex social structures; they do not understand the workings of adult minds, and cannot address difficult political and religious issues. The need to list and memorise 'causes and effects' killed school history for many people and there is still a danger that teachers will over-interpret the content specified in the revised curriculum.

Experience suggests that children are interested in detail, and in problem-solving in which they can be validly and genuinely engaged: what did sailors on the Armada ships eat? What did the sailors on the *Mary Rose* do? Who lived in my home before I did?

Therefore, the curriculum must be taught in an economical way if it is not to be overloaded. Planning must be carefully focused to centre on real problem-solving in each curriculum area, and in a range of contexts. Planning, activities and evaluation must form a related sequence so that assessment is an integral part of all the work children do and of the constant interaction between teacher and child. Work planned in history must reflect the thinking processes of history, and allow for a range of differentiated outcomes. It should also involve learning history through the rich variety of activities on which good primary practice is based:

- information technology (simulations, word-processing and data-handling);
- art (drawing, printing, painting, embroidery, modelmaking);
- science and technology (cooking, spinning, weaving, grinding seeds, building and testing structures, using tools, moving loads, using a range of materials);
- language for different audiences (transactional and expressive writing, reading, discussion, role-play, making video and audio tapes).

In conclusion

There are many opportunities to interpret the new framework for history in creative ways, planning activities which reflect an increased understanding of the nature of history, an articulate rationale for its importance, and the sharing of teachers' own enthusiasms. Nevertheless, the position of history in the curriculum is probably more precarious than before. The statutory requirement is minimal, with a recognition that some outline studies are inevitable; on the other hand, there is increasing emphasis on tests in 'basic skills' and on published league tables of the results. Yet

> The present is where we get lost
> If we forget our own past and have
> No vision of the future.
>
> (Ayi Kwei Amah in Fryer 1988)

Whether or not this is allowed to happen will depend on the enthusiasm, efforts and expertise of all those who care about primary history, working together with conviction. This will involve convincing parents of the importance of history, if they are to understand, value and support it; involving them in visits and follow-up work, in collecting resources, organising school museums, collections, contributing to oral history, providing informed audiences for, or participating in presentations.

For this reason, one school always begins a term by inviting parents to a meeting at which work planned is explained: what the children will be doing, how and why.

A mother became sufficiently interested to watch a television programme about excavations at a Celtic hill fort which she talked about over breakfast the following morning with her eight-year-old son. 'But Mum,' he asked, 'what is the evidence for that?' Another child, after a school visit to Canterbury Cathedral, took her grandparents on an informed investigation of their local cathedral in Norwich. If parents and guardians become involved in their children's work in history they understand the kinds of thinking this requires and can share in and respond to evaluations of topic books, presentations and models, so that summative, end of key stage assessment is meaningful and valued.

Professionals also need to support each other if history is to be seen as an important and valued part of the primary curriculum. Class teachers remain the key practitioners, but they are increasingly working with educators in museums and galleries, and in partnership with colleagues in higher education, to investigate new approaches through action research, as roles in teacher education change.

Education, like history, is a dynamic process and teachers are resilient and resourceful people who will surely respond – again – to the challenges ahead.

Both continuity and change in primary history education over the last decade are illustrated throughout this third edition. There is no doubt the process will continue.

Appendix

History Internet Sites Referred to in the Text

Anne Frank Online – http://www.annefrank.com
A fascinating photo scrapbook accompanying the story of Anne's life with her family – selected extracts from her diary and a tour of the rooms where Anne lived for two years, a brief history of the Holocaust and an education and schools section.

**The Aztecs (Snaith Primary School) –
http://home.freeuk.net/elloughton13/aztecs.htm**
An award-winning site attractively written for children but with lots of teaching notes and printable booklets. There are stories to read, ancient writing to decode and pictures of artefacts and temples, etc. Pupils are also encouraged to study the archaeological and 'written' evidence left by the Aztecs.

A Walk Through Time – http://www.bbc.co.uk/education/walk/
A history website for 7–9 year-olds.

BBC Education – http://www.bbc.co.uk/education/history/index.shtml
Expanding website – time-line of British history from 4000 BC to present day to be included soon. Covers many National Curriculum topics and includes articles, quizzes and links to BBC history programmes. Excellent web links to history education sites – with evaluations.

**BBC guide to education on the web –
http://db.bbc.co.uk/education_webguide/pkg main.p home**
An invaluable site. It has a section of 187 history websites for primary education and 160 for secondary – all with comprehensive evaluations.

**BBC Timelines England and Scotland –
http://www.bbc.co.uk/education/history/timelines.shtml**

BBC History 2000 project offers these multilevel time-lines of the histories of England and Scotland from the Neolithic age to the present. As time-lines go, these are unusually detailed and provide paragraph-length descriptions, often accompanied by photos, artwork or 3-D online models about events and personalities such as the building of Hadrian's Wall, Lady Jane Grey and Robert the Bruce.

Compose World Junior is available from: ESP Music, 21 Beech Lane, West Hallam, Ilkeston, Derbyshire DE7 6GP

English Heritage – http://www.english-heritage.org.uk
Very good site – includes the archaeology division which now has the updated version of 'Virtual Stonehenge'. It also has details of all English Heritage places to visit, time trails, special events, etc. Also provides access to the National Monuments Record with its millions of aerial photographs and photographs of buildings from the 1850s to the present, and covering the whole country.

**Forum Romanum –
http://www.geocities.com.Athens/Forum/6946/rome.html**
Ideal for KS2 pupils, this vast site includes a virtual rout of Rome, a dictionary of mythology, picture index and lots of information, images and links on the culture, language and history of Ancient Rome.

**The Greeks –
http://www.pbs.org/empires/thegreeks/htmlver/index.html**
Extensive website with masses of information on Greek history.

Harrappa (History of South Asia) – http://www.harappa.com/
Good section on the Indus Valley including a 90-slide tour with script, essays and information.

**History web links –
http://www.liv/ac/uk/~evansjon/humanities/history/history.html**
Good page on education links for students and teachers. This site is being updated constantly.

***Local History* magazine – http://www.local-history.co.uk**
Useful site – gives information on the Local History magazine but also tips on getting started in local history plus lots of related websites and useful addresses.

The London Blitz – http://www.pnc.com.au~insight/blitz/blitz.html

A comprehensive website describing how Londoners lived and survived during the Blitz. It is equally relevant to Coventry, Liverpool, etc. and covers topics including rationing, evacuation, defence services, the blackout and coping in wartime. It combines information, facts and figures, personal accounts and original photographs to produce a very full and interesting website.

**Mark Millmore's Ancient Egypt –
http://eyelid.ukonline.co.uk/ancient/egypt.htm**

Pyramids and temples, kings and queens, hieroglyphs resources, games and a section on Egyptian mathematics. Masses of information with excellent pictures and a very good links section.

National Grid for Learning – www.ngfl.gov.uk

A portal site accessing an increasing range of materials of interest to history teachers.

**Public Records Office – Learning Curve Gallery –
http://www/pro/gov.uk/education/snapshots/default.htm**

Excellent site – offers a series of cross-reference 'snapshots' from the past. Original historical sources are accompanied by questions and activities aimed at KS2–4. (Teaching notes are included.)

Spartacus Educational – http://www/spartacus.schoolnet.co.uk

Lots of information on themes from 18th, 19th and 20th century, including railways, World War I, Vietnam and the emancipation of women. There is a free encyclopaedia with over 1000 entries, covering social and political history.

**Tudor England for KS2 teachers and pupils –
http://tudor.simplenet.com/**

Lots of pictures of the Tudor monarchs and also information on many aspects of Tudor life.

20th Century Vox – http://www.bbc.co.uk/education/20cvox/

A BBC website giving you all the information needed to run an oral history project. Audio archives on a wide variety of subjects – useful resource.

General History Websites

Home page for BBC Education – http://www.bbc.co.uk/education/home

**CADW Welsh Historic Monuments –
http://www.castlewales.com/cadw.html/**
Comprehensive guide, lots of photographs and detailed information.

Globe Theatres – http://www.reading.ac.uk/globe/
Much detail on the history of the Globe Theatres and the staging of the Shakespeare plays.

H-Net academic network – http://www.h-net.msu.edu/

Historic Scotland – http://www.historic-scotland.gov.uk/
Sections on heritage, visitor attractions, education, questions and links, etc.

History Channel site – http://www.thehistorychannel.co.uk/index.htm

MuseumNet – http://www.museums.co.uk
A comprehensive listing of UK museums, including information on exhibits and visiting hours, plus e-mail addresses and direct links to museum websites.

National Gallery – http://www.nationalgallery/org.uk/
Collections now available online, with details of current exhibitions, etc.

Public Record Office site – http://www.pro.gov.uk/

Spartacus educational website – http://www.spartacus.schoolnet.co.uk

**Teachers Evaluating Educational Multimedia site –
http://www.teem.org.uk**

Tate Gallery – http://www.tate.org.uk/
Collections, library and archives can now be browsed online.

Useful for history site links – http://www.yahoo.co.uk

**Virtual Teachers Centre site –
http://www.vtc.nglf.gov.uk/resource/cits/history/index.html**

**Offers a variety of history links –
http://schools.channel4.com/online_resources/index.html**

Places to Visit: Museums, Galleries

English Heritage – http://www.english-heritage.org.uk. (*see above*)

Museums – http://www.comlab.ox.ac.uk/archive/other/museums
Gives details of many museums and places of interest around the world.

The Victorian Web – http://landow.stg.brown.edu/victorian/victor.html
A very comprehensive site covering all aspects of Victorian life, including religion technology, the visual arts, literature, social history, etc.

The Viking Network Web – http://viking.no/
A lot of information about the Vikings although it is mainly text based; quizzes and Viking games and a chance for schools to become involved and contribute.

The Wonders of Ancient Egypt –
http://www.geocities.com/Athens/Delphi/3499/page1.htm
Suitable for KS2 pupils. Sections on the Great Pyramid, the Sphinx and a virtual tour of Tutankhamun's Tomb. Also secrets of mummification. Children would enjoy this site.

References

Alderson, (ed.) (1975) *A Book of Bosh, Edward Lear.* Harmondsworth: Kestrel Books/Penguin.

Arnold, H. and Slater, L. (1999) *Victorians (9–11).* Reading for Information Series. Leamington Spa: Scholastic.

Arthur, J. and Phillips, R. (eds) (2000) *Issues in the Teaching of History.* London: Routledge.

Ashby, R. and Lee, P. J. (1987) 'Children's Concepts of Empathy and Understanding in History', in C. Portal (ed.) *The History Curriculum for Teachers.* Lewes: Falmer Press.

Ausubel, D. P. (1963) *The Psychology of Meaningful Verbal Learning.* New York: Grunea Stratton.

Ausubel, D. P. (1968) *Educational Psychology.* A Cognitive View. London: Holt, Rinehart and Winston.

Bage, G. (1999) *Narrative Matters. Teaching and Learning History through Story.* Lewes: Falmer Press.

Bage, G., Lister, B. and Grisdale, R. (1999) *Classical History in Primary Schools, Teaching and Learning at Key Stage 2.* London: QCA Publications.

Barnes, D. and Todd, F. (1977) *Communication and Learning in Small Groups.* London: Routledge and Kegan Paul.

Bawden, N. (1973) *Carrie's War.* London: Victor Gollancz.

Beard, R. M. (1960) 'The Nature and Development of Concepts', *Educational Review* **13**(1): 12–26.

Beddoe, D. (1983) *Discovering Women's History.* London: Pandora.

Belloc, H. (1991) *Matilda, Who Told Lies and Was Burned to Death.* London: Red Fox.

Bennett, N. and Dunne, E. (1992) *Managing Classroom Groups.* London: Simon and Schuster.

Bernot, L. and Blancard, R. (1953) *Nouville, un Village Francis.* Paris: Institut d'Ethnologie.

Bersu, G. (1940) *Excavations at Little Woodbury,* Part 1. Proceedings of the Historic Society, 6, pp. 30–111.

Biott, C. (1984) *Getting on Without the Teacher. Primary School Pupils in Cooperative*

Groups. Collaborative Research Paper 1. Sunderland Polytechnic. Schools Council Programme Two.

Black, M. (1992) *The Medieval Cookbook.* London: British Museum Press.

Blakeway, S. E. (1983) 'Some Aspects of the Historical Understanding of Children aged 7 to 11'. Unpubl. MA Dissertation. London University Institute of Education.

Blyth, A. (1990) *Making the Grade for Primary Humanities.* Milton Keynes: Open University Press.

Blyth, J. E. (1988) *History 5–9.* London: Hodder and Stoughton.

Blyth, J. and Hughes, P. (1997) *Using Written Sources in Primary History.* London: Hodder and Stoughton.

Booth, M. B. (1969) *History Betrayed.* London: Longmans, Green and Co.

Booth, M. (1979) 'A Longitudinal Study of the Cognitive Skills, Concepts and Attitudes of Adolescents Studying a Modern World History Syllabus, and an Analysis of their Historical Thinking'. Unpubl. Ph.D. Thesis. University of Reading.

Borke, H. (1978) 'Piaget's View of Social Interaction and the Theoretical Construct of Empathy', in L. E. Siegal and C. J. Brainerd (eds) *Alternatives to Piaget.* London: Academic Press.

Boulding, E. (1976) *Handbook of International Data on Women.* Beverley Hills: Sage.

Boulding, E. (1977) *Women in the Twentieth Century World.* New York: Sage.

Boulding, G. E. (1981) *The Underside of History.* Boulder, Co.:Westview.

Bradley, N. C. (1947) 'The Growth of the Knowledge of Time in Children of School Age', *British Journal of Psychology* **38**: 67–8.

Brown, G. and Wragg. E. C. (1993) *Questioning.* London: Routledge.

Bruner, J. S. (1963) *The Process of Education.* New York: Vintage Books.

Bruner, J. S. (1966) *Towards a Theory of Instruction*, 7th edn. 1975. Harvard, Mass.: The Belknapp Press of Harvard University Press.

Bruner, J. (1996) *The Culture of Education.* Cambridge, Mass.: Harvard University Press.

Buck, M., Sally, I. and Moorse, K. (1994) *Educating the Whole Child: Crosscurricular Themes Within the History Curriculum*, Occasional Paper 10. London: The Historical Association.

Butterworth, G. and Light, P. (1982) (eds) *Social Cognition – Studies in the Development of Understanding.* Brighton: Harvester Press.

Claire, H. (1996) *Reclaiming Our Pasts: equality and diversity in the primary curriculum.* London: Trentham Books.

Clarke, R. R. (1960) *East Anglia.* London: Thames and Hudson.

Collingwood, R. G. (1939) *An Autobiography* (paperback 1970). London: Oxford University Press.

Coltham, J. (1960) 'Junior School Children's Understanding of Historical Terms'. Unpubl. Ph.D. Thesis. University of Manchester.

Cooper, H. J. (1991) 'Young Children's Thinking in History'. Unpubl. Ph.D. Thesis. London University Institute of Education.

Cooper, H. (1993) 'Removing the Scaffolding: A Case Study Investigating How Whole-class Teaching can lead to Effective Peer Group Discussion Without the Teacher', *Curriculum Journal* **4**(3): 385–401.

Cooper, H. (1994) in Hilary Bourdillon (ed.) *Teaching History*, Chs 5 and 8. London: Routledge.

Cooper, H. (1995a) *The Teaching of History in Primary Schools*, 2nd edn. London: David Fulton Publishers.

Cooper, H. (1995b) *History in the Early Years*. London: Routledge.

Cooper, H. (1996) 'Exploring Links between Whole Class Teaching and Small Group Discussion', TOPIC, No. 15. Slough: National Foundation for Educational Research.

Cooper, H. (1997) 'History in its Own Write', *Primary English Magazine* 3(2): 14–17.

Cooper, H. (1998a) 'History in its Own Write (2)', *Primary English Magazine* 3(3): 16–18.

Cooper, H. (1998b) 'Writing about History in the Early Years', in P. Hoodless (ed.) *History and English in the Primary School*, pp. 157–78. London: Routledge.

Cooper, H. and Etches, P. (1996) 'Church Going-Kendal', *Teaching History* **83**: 30–4.

Cooper, H. and Twiselton, S. (1998) 'Victorian Alphabets: a sampler for the Literacy Hour?', *Primary English Magazine* 4(2): 7–11.

Cooper, H. and Twiselton, S. (1999) 'Victorian Alphabets: a sample for the Literacy Hour (2)', *Primary English Magazine* 4(3): 18–21.

Cooper, H. and Twiselton, S. (2000) *Art and Artists: Impressionism (7–9)*. Reading for Information Series. Leamington Spa: Scholastic.

Corbishley, M. and Cooper, M. (1999) *Real Romans Real Castles, Real Victorians*. London: English Heritage TAG Publishing.

Council of Europe, Strasburg (1995). Council of Europe Council for Cultural Cooperation: Meeting of experts on educational research, on the learning and teaching of history. Strasbourg 19–20 June 1995.

Counsell, C. and Thomson, K. (1997) *Life in Tudor Times*, Cambridge Primary History Series. Cambridge: Cambridge University Press.

Counsell, C. (1997) *Analytical and Discussive Writing at Key Stage 3*. London: The Historical Association.

Cowie, E. E. (1985) *History and the Slow Learning Child*. Teaching History Series No. 41. London: The Historical Association.

Cox, M. V. (ed.) (1986) *The Development of Cognition and Language*. Brighton: Harvester Press.

Crowther, E. (1982) 'Understanding of the Concept of Change among Children and Young Adolescents', *Educational Review* **34**(3): 279–84.

Croydon and Stockport Workhouse. Community Information Resource Project (1989) Davidson Professional Centre. Croydon.

Curtis, R. and Elton, B. (1999) *Blackadder: The Whole Damn Dynasty*. Harmondsworth: Penguin.

Da Silva, W. A. (1969) 'Concept Formation in History through Conceptual Clues'. Unpubl. Ph.D. Thesis. University of Birmingham.

David, R. (1996) *History at Home*. London: English Heritage.

Davidson, B. (1997) *Picturing the Past*. London: English Heritage.

Davies, R. (1998) 'Why is history essential?', *Welsh Historian* **28**: 4–5.

Davies, J. and Redmond, J. (1998) *Coordinating History across the Primary School*. London: Falmer Press.

Davis, J. (1986) *Artefacts in the Primary School.* Teaching History Series. No. 45, p. 8. London: The Historical Association.

Department for Education and Employment (1995a) *History in the National Curriculum.* London: HMSO.

Department for Education and Employment (1995b) *Key Stages 1 and 2 of the National Curriculum.* London: HMSO.

Department for Education and Employment (1998a) *The National Literacy Strategy Literacy.* London: DfEE.

Department for Education and Employment (1998b) *Teaching: High Status, High Standards. Requirements for Courses in Initial Teacher Training.* London: Teacher Training Agency.

Department for Education and Employment (1999a) *The National Numeracy Strategy.* London: DfEE.

Department for Education and Employment (1999b) *The National Curriculum for England* (www.nc.uk.net).

Department of Education and Science (1978) Primary Education in England and Wales; Survey by Her Majesty's Inspector of Schools. London: HMSO.

Department of Education and Science (1982) *Education 5–9.* London: HMSO.

Department of Education and Science (1983) *9–13 Middle Schools: An Illustrative Survey.* London: HMSO.

Department of Education and Science (1989) *The Teaching and Learning of History and Geography.* London: HMSO.

Department of Education and Science (1991a) *History in the National Curriculum.* London: HMSO.

Dickinson, A. K. and Lee, P. J. (1978) (eds) *History Teaching and Historical Understanding.* London: Heinemann.

Dickinson, A. and Lee, P. J. (1994) 'Investigating Progression in Children's Ideas about History: The CHATA Project', in Partnership and Progress, New Developments in History Teacher Education and History Teaching, pp. 78–101. USDE Papers in Education, University of Sheffield.

Doise, W. (1978) *Groups and Individuals: Explanations in Social Psychology.* Cambridge: Cambridge University Press.

Doise, W., Mugny, C. and Perret Clermont, A. N. (1975) 'Social Interaction and the Development of Cognitive Operations', *European Journal of Social Psychology* **5**: 367–83.

Doise, W. and Mugny, G. (1979) 'Individual and Collective Conflicts of Centrations in Cognitive Development', *European Journal of Social Psychology* **9**: 105–9.

Donaldson, M. (1978) *Children's Minds.* London: Fontana.

Ellerington, C. (1997) *The History and Politics of Oral Traditions in the English Nursery.* Ph.D. in progress, University of Cardiff.

Elton, G. R. (1970) 'What Sort of History Should we Teach?', in M. Ballard (ed.) *New Movements in the Study and Teaching of History.* London: Temple Smith.

English Heritage (1998a) *Story Telling at Historic Sites.* Northampton: English Heritage.

English Heritage (1998b) *A Teacher Guide to Maths and the Historic Environment.*

London: English Heritage.

Erikson, E. H. (1965) *Childhood and Society*. Harmondsworth: Penguin.

Ernest, E. (1968) *The Kate Greenaway Treasury*. London: Collins.

European Conference of Educational Research, Frankfurt (1997), 24–27 September 1997.

Famous Sailors (1970) London: Macdonald.

Ferguson, J., Montgomerie, D. and Price, M. (1995) *History – Studying the Facts, a National Curriculum Project for Key Stage 2 Linking History, Drama and English*. The Young Historian Scheme Leaflet No. 2. London: The Historical Association.

Fines, J. and Nichol, J. (1997) *Teaching Primary History*. Oxford: Heinemann.

Flavell, J. H. (1985) *Cognitive Development*, 2nd edn. London and New York: Prentice Hall.

Fleming, K. (1992) 'A Land Fit for Heroes: Recreating the Past through Drama', *Teaching History* **68**: 14–16.

Foreman, M. (1995) *After the War is Over*. London: Pallion.

Frank, A. (1989) *The Diary of Anne Frank*. London: Pan Books.

Freedman, J. L. and Loftus, E. F. (1971) 'Retrieval of Words from Long-Term Memory', *Journal of Verbal Learning and Verbal Behaviour* **10**: 107–15.

Friedman, K.C. (1978) 'Time Concepts of Elementary School Children', *Elementary School Journal* **44**: 337–42.

Fryer, P. (1984) *Staying Power*. London: Pluto Press.

Fryer, P. (1989) *Black People in the British Empire – An Introduction*. London: Pluto Press.

Furth, H. G. (1980) *The World of Grown Ups*. New York: Elsevier.

Gagne, R. M. (1977) *The Conditions of Learning*. London: Holt, Rinehart and Winston.

Galton, M., and Williamson, J. (1992) *Group Work in the Primary School*. London: Routledge.

Garfield, L. and Blishen, E. (1970) *The God Beneath the Sea*. London: Longman.

Garvey, C. (1977) *Play*. The Developing Child Series. London: Collins/Fontana.

Georg Eckert Institut, Brunswick (1998) Education for International Understanding: What do we know about pupils' historical consciousness, and geographical awareness and the role of textbooks in teaching history, geography and civics? UNESCO Conference, 8–10 June 1998.

Gerrard, R. (1998) Sir Francis Drake, his Daring Deeds. Harmondsworth: Puffin.

Getzels, J. W. and Jackson, P. W. (1962) *Creativity and Intelligence: Explorations with Students*. London and New York: Wiley.

Gittings, C. (1991) 'Portraits as Historical Evidence in the Primary School', in *Primary History Today*. London: The Historical Association.

Goldstein, A. P. and Michels, G. Y. (1985) *Empathy: Developmental Training and Consequences*. Hillsdale NJ: Lawrence Erlbaum Associates.

Green, J. (1992) *Native Peoples of the Americas*. Oxford: Oxford University Press

Guilford, J. P. (1959) 'Traits of Creativity', in H. H. Anderson (ed.) *Creativity and Its Cultivation*, pp. 142–61. New York: Harper and Row.

Haddon, F. A. and Lytton, H. (1968) 'Teaching Approach and the Development of Divergent Thinking Abilities in Primary Schools', *British Journal of Educational*

Psychology **38**: June 1968 171–80.

Hallam, R. N. (1975) 'A Study of the Effect of Teaching Method on the Growth of Logical Thought, with Special Reference to the Teaching of History using Criteria from Piaget's Theory of Cognitive Development'. Unpubl. Ph.D. Thesis. University of Leeds.

Hamel, K. (2000) 'The Odyssey: a Musical and Historical Journey', *Primary History* **24**: 6–7.

Hamlyn, D. (1982) 'What Exactly is Social about the Origins of Understanding?', in G. Butterworth and P. Light (eds) *Social Cognition: Studies in the Development of Understanding*. Brighton: Harvester Press.

Harding, D. W. (1974) *The Iron Age in Lowland Britain*. London: Routledge and Kegan Paul.

Harner, L. (1982) 'Talking about the Past and the Future', in W. Friedman (ed.) *The Developmental Psychology of Time*. New York: Academic Press.

Harnett, P. (1993) 'Identifying Progression in Children's Understanding; the use of Visual Materials to assess primary school children's learning in history', *Cambridge Journal of Education* **23**(2): 137–54.

Harpin, W. (1976) *The Second 'R': Writing Development in the Junior School*. London: Allen and Unwin.

Haydn, T. (1999) 'Information and Communications Technology in the History Classroom', in J. Arthur and R. Phillips (eds) *Issues in Teaching History*. London: Routledge.

Hayes: QCA (1998) *Can do Better: raising boys' achievement in English*. Hayes, Middlesex: Qualification and Curriculum Authority.

Hill, C. (1980) *The World Turned Upside Down: Radical Ideas during the English Revolution*. Harmondsworth: Penguin.

Hodgkinson, K. (1986) 'How Artefacts can Stimulate Historical Thinking in Young Children', *Education 3–13* **14**(2): 14–17.

Hoodless, P. (1996) *Time and Timelines in the Primary School*. London: The Historical Association.

Hoodless, P. (ed.) (1998) *History and English in the Primary School*. London: Routledge.

Huggins, M. (2000) '1066 and All That! Pupils' Misconceptions in History', in H. Cooper and R. Hyland (eds) *Children's Perceptions of Learning with Trainee Teachers*. London: Routledge.

Hulton, M. (1989 'African Traditional Stories in the Classroom', in D. Atkinson (ed.) *The Children's Bookroom: Reading and the Use of Books*. Stoke on Trent: Trentham.

Hunt, M. (2000) 'Teaching Historical Significance', in J. Arthur and R. Phillips (eds) *Issues in Teaching History*. London: Routledge.

Husbands, C. (1996) *What is History Teaching? Language, Ideas and Meaning in Learning about the Past*. Buckingham: Open University Press.

Hutchins, P. (1973) *Rosie's Walk*. London: Picture Puffins.

Institut National de Recherche Pedagogique, Paris (1996) Concepts, Modèles, Raisonnements. Huitieme Colloque (2–29 March 1996).

Isaacs, S. (1948) *Intellectual Growth in Young Children*. London: Routledge and Kegan Paul.

Jahoda, G. (1963) 'Children's Concept of Time and History', *Educational Review* **15**: 87–104.

Jenkins, K. (1995) *On 'What is History?' from Carr and Elton to Rorty and White.* London: Routledge.

Jones, R. M. (1968) *Fantasy and Feeling in Education.* London: London University Press.

Kerry, T. (1998) *Questioning and Explaining in Classrooms.* London: Hodder & Stoughton.

Kitson Clarke, G. (1967) *The Critical Historian.* London: Heinemann.

Klausmeier, H. J. and Allen, P. S. (1978) *Cognitive Development of Children and Youth. A Longitudinal Study.* London: Academic Press.

Klausmeier, H. J. *et al.* (1979) *Cognitive Learning and Development.* Cambridge, Mass.: Ballinger.

Knight, P. (1989a) 'Children's Understanding of People in the Past'. Unpubl. Ph.D. Thesis. University of Lancaster.

Knight, P. (1989b) 'Empathy: Concept, Confusion and Consequences in a National Curriculum', *Oxford Review of Education* **15**(1): 41–53.

Knight, P. (1989c) 'A Study of Children's Understanding of People in the Past', *Educational Review* **41**(3): 207–19.

Lawton, D. (1975) *Class, Culture and the Curriculum.* London: Routledge and Kegan Paul.

Leach, E. (1973) 'Some Anthropological Observations on Number, Time and Common Sense', in G. A. Howson (ed.) *Developments in Mathematical Education.* Cambridge: Cambridge University Press.

Lee. P. J. *et al.* (1998) 'History in an Information Culture', paper given at the Symposium, Teaching and Learning as Epistemic Acts, American Educational Research Association Conference, San Diego, California.

Lee, P. J. *et al.* (1996a) 'There were no facts in those days: children's ideas about historical explanation' in M. Hughes (ed.) *Teaching and Learning in Changing Times.* Oxford: Blackwell.

Lee, P. J. *et al.* (1996b) 'Children Making Sense of History', *Education 3–13* **24**(1):13–19.

Lee, P. J. *et al.* (1996c) 'Progression in Children's Ideas about History', in M. Hughes (ed.) *Progression in Children's Learning.* Clevedon, Bristol (PA) and Adelaide: Multilingual Matters.

Lee, P. J. *et al.* (1996d), 'Children's Understanding of "because" and the Status of Explanation in History', *Teaching History* **82**(1): 6–11.

Lello, J. (1980) 'The Concept of Time, the Teaching of History and School Organisation', *History Teacher* **13**(3): 341–50.

Lewis, M. and Wray, D. (1988), 'Bringing Literacy and History Closer Together', *Primary History* **20**: 11–13.

Light, P. (1986) 'The Social Concomitants of Role-Taking', in M. V. Cox (ed.), *The Development of Cognition and Language.* Brighton: Harvester Press.

Little, V. (1989) 'Imagination and History', in J. Campbell and V. Little (eds) *Humanities in the Primary School.* Lewes: Falmer Press.

Lomas, T. (1994) *A Guide to Preparing the History Curriculum in Primary Schools, for an OFSTED Inspection.* London: The Historical Association.

Lomas, T. (1999) 'The Historical Association's response to the Curriculum 2000 proposals', *Primary History* **23**: 5.

Lynn, S. (1993) 'Children Reading Pictures: History Visuals at Key Stages 1 and 2', *Education 3–13* **21**(3): 23–9.

Macdonald, F. and Wood, G. (1999) *Ancient African Town – Benin.* London: Franklin Watts.

Marbeau, L. (1988) 'History and Geography in School', *Primary Education* **88**(2): 26–42.

Martin, D. and Cobb, A. (1992) 'Evacuation Day', *Primary History* **2**: 7–8.

Martin, R. B. (1980) *Tennyson, The Unquiet Heart.* Oxford: Oxford University Press.

Matar, N. (1999) *Turks, Moors and Englishmen in the Age of Discovery.* Columbia: Columbia University Press.

McAleavy, T. (1997) (series ed.) *Cambridge Primary History.* Cambridge: Cambridge University Press.

McCraughrean, G. (1999) *Britannia: 100 Great Stories from British History.* London: Orion.

McEwan, I. (1985) *Rose Blanche.* London: Jonathan Cape.

Merriman, N. (1990) Curator, Museum of London in *The Times*, 23 August 1990.

Mink, L. O. (1968) 'Collingwood's Dialectic of History', *History and Theory* **VII**(1): 3–37.

Mitchell, R. and Middleton. G. (1967) *Living History Book One.* Edinburgh: Holmes McDougall.

Moyles, J. R. (1989) *Just Playing? The Role and Status of Play in Early Childhood Education.* Milton Keynes: Open University Press.

National Curriculum for History, Final Report (1990). National Curriculum History Working Group Final Report. Department of Education and Science and Welsh Office.

National Oracy Project (1992) (ed.) Kate Norman. *Thinking Voices. The Work of the National Oracy Project.* London: Hodder and Stoughton.

Newman, E. and Turpin, D. (1997) 'Spicing the National Curriculum: the Romans and the Spice Trade, a theme for an ethnically diverse primary school', *Primary History* **15**: 8–10.

Nichol, J. (1998) 'Nuffield Primary History: The Literacy Through History Project and The Literacy Hour', *Primary History* **20**: 14–17.

Nichol, J. (2000) 'Literacy, Text Genres and History: Reading and Learning from Difficult and Challenging Texts', *Primary History* **24**: 13–17.

Nichol, J. and Dean, J. (1997) *History 7–11: developing primary teaching skills.* London: Routledge.

Noble, P. (1986) *The 17th Century.* London: Ward Lock Educational.

Norton, M. (1999) 'Making the Most of ICT at Key Stage 2', *Primary History* **21**: 79.

Office for Standards in Education (1999) *Primary Education 1994–98: A Review of Primary Schools in England.* London: OFSTED.

Opie, I. and Opie, P. (eds) (1973) *The Oxford Book of Children's Verse.* Oxford: Clarendon.

Opie, I. and Opie, P. (1980) *The Nursery Companion.* Oxford: Oxford University Press.

Osler, A. (1995) 'Does the National Curriculum bring us any Closer to a Gender Balanced

History?', *Teaching History* **79**: 21–4.

Parnes, S. H. (1959) *Instructor's Manual for Semester Courses in Creative Problem-Solving*. Buffalo. New York: Creative Education Foundation.

Peel, E. A. (1960) *The Pupil's Thinking*. London: Oldbourne.

Peel, E. A. (1967) in M. H. Burston and D. Thompson (eds) *Studies in the Nature and Teaching of History*. London: Routledge.

Phenix, P. (1964) *Realms of Meaning*. New York: McGraw Hill.

Phillips, R. (1998) *History Teaching, Nationhood and the State: A Study in Educational Policies*. London: Cassell.

Phillips, R. (1999) 'History and English in the Primary School: Exploiting the Links', reviewed in *Primary History* **23:** 21.

Piaget, J. (1926) *The Language and Thought of the Child* (3rd edn 1959). London: Routledge.

Piaget, J. (1928) *Judgement and Reasoning in the Child*. London: Kegan Paul.

Piaget, J. (1932) *Moral Judgement and the Child*. London: Kegan Paul.

Piaget, J. (1950) *The Psychology of Intelligence*. London: Routledge and Kegan Paul.

Piaget, J. (1952) *The Child's Conception of Number*. London: Routledge.

Piaget, J. (1969) *A Children's Concept of Time*. London: Routledge and Kegan Paul.

Piaget, J. and Inhelder, B. (1951) *The Origin of the Idea of Chance in the Child*. London: Routledge.

Pocock, T. (1974) *Nelson and His World*. London: Thames and Hudson.

Pocock, T. (1987) *Horatio Nelson*. London: Bodley Head.

Pounce, E. (1995) 'Ensuring Continuity and Understanding through Teaching of Gender Issues in History 5–16', in R. Watts and I. Grosvenor (eds), *Crossing the Key Stages of History*. London: David Fulton Publishers.

Pring, R. (1976) *Knowledge and Schooling*. Wells: Open Books.

Prisk, T. (1987) 'Letting Them Get On With It: A Study of an Unsupervised Group Task in an Infant School', in A. Pollard, *Children and their Primary Schools*. Lewes: Falmer Press.

Qualifications and Curriculum Authority (1998a) *Maintaining Balance and Breadth at Key Stages 1 and 2*. London: QCA.

Qualifications and Curriculum Authority/Department for Education and Employment (1998b) *History Teacher's Guide: A Scheme of Work for Key Stages 1 and 2*. London: QCA.

Qualifications and Curriculum Authority (1999) *The Early Learning Goals*. London: QCA, www.qca.org.uk.

Qualification and Curriculum Authority/Department for Education and Employment (2000) *Update of History Schemes of Work*. London: QCA.

Rees, A. (1976) 'Teaching Strategies for the Advancement and Development of Thinking Skills in History. Unpubl. M.Phil. Thesis. University of London.

Richmond, I. A. (1955) *Roman Britain*. Harmondsworth: Penguin.

Richmond, J. (1982) *The Resources of Classroom Language*. London: Arnold.

Riley, C. (1999) Evidential Understanding, period knowledge and the development of literacy: a practical approach to layers of inference for Key Stage 3, *Teaching History* **97**: 6–12.

Roberts, F. (1992) *India 1526–1800*. London: Hodder and Stoughton.

Roberts, N. (1998) *Literacy Hour Resources*. Wisbech: Nicholas Roberts Publications.

Robinson, T. (1999) *Kings and Queens*. London: Hutchinson.

Robson, E. R. (1874) *School Architecture* (republished in 1972, with introduction by M. Seaborne). Leicester: Leicester University Press.

Rodney, W. (1972) *How Europe Underdeveloped Africa*. London: L'Ouverture Bogle.

Rogers, R. C. (1959) 'Towards a Theory of Creativity', in H. H. Anderson (ed.) *Creativity and its Cultivation*. New York: Harper and Row.

Rosen, C. and Rosen, H. (1973) *The Language of Primary School Children*. Harmondsworth: Penguin.

Rowbotham, S. (1973) *Hidden from History*. London: Pluto.

Rowse, A. L. (1946) *The Use of History*. London: Hodder and Stoughton.

Ruddock, J. (1979) *Learning to Teach Through Discussion*. C.A.R.E. University of East Anglia.

Russell, J. (1981) 'Why "Socio-Cognitive Conflict" May be Impossible: The Status of Egocentric Errors in the Dyadic Performance of a Spatial Task', *Education Psychology* **1**: 159–69.

Ryle, G. (1979) *On Thinking*. Oxford: Blackwell.

Sampson, B. (ed.) (1977) *Edward Lear: An Alphabet*. The Windmill Press.

Sampson, J., Grugeon, L. and Yiannaki, E. (1998) 'Learning the Language of History; teaching subject specific language and concepts', in P. Hoodless (ed.), *History and English in the Primary School*. London: Routledge.

Schools Council (1976–1978) *History 13–16*. Edinburgh: Holmes McDougall.

Schools Council (1979) *Learning through Talking 11–16*. London: Evans/Methuen Educational.

Schools Council (1983) *Akbar and Elizabeth*. London: Schools Council Publications.

Schools Curriculum and Assessment Authority (1995) *Planning the Curriculum at Key Stages 1 and 2*. London: SCAA.

Schools Curriculum and Assessment Authority (1997) *Planning the Curriculum at Key Stages 1 and 2*. London: SCAA.

Schools Curriculum and Assessment Authority. *Can do Better: Gender in English*. London: SCAA.

SEAC (1993) *Children's Work Assessed: History and Geography*. London: HMSO.

Sebba, J. (1994) *History for All*. London: David Fulton Publishers.

Sellars, W. C. and Yeatman, R. J. (1973) *1066 and all That*. Harmondsworth: Penguin.

Sendak, M. (1970) *Where the Wild Things Are*. Harmondsworth: Penguin.

Shawyer, G., Booth, M. and Brown, R. (1988) 'The Development of Children's Historical Thinking', *Cambridge Journal of Education* **18**(2): 209–20.

Shemilt, D. (1980) *History 13–16 Evaluation Study*. Edinburgh: Holmes McDougall.

Sherwood, M. (1997) 'Key Stage 2 multicultural issues', *Teaching History* **87**: 23–6.

Shif, Zh. (1935) *The Development of Scientific and Everyday Concepts*. Moscow: Uchpedgiz.

Smart, L. (1999) 'Any place for a database in the teaching and learning of history at Key Stage 1?', *Primary History* **23**: 8–10.

Smith, L. N. and Tomlinson, P. (1977) 'The Development of Children's Construction of Historical Duration', *Educational Research* **19**(3): 163–70.

Smith, N. (1992) *Black Peoples of the Americas*. Oxford: Oxford University Press.

Speed, P. and Speed, M. (1987) *The Elizabethan Age, Book 1*. Oxford: Oxford University Press.

Stones, E. (1979) *Psychopedagogy* (Ch. 9). London and New York: Methuen.

Stow, W. (2000) 'Issues in the Teaching of Chronology', in J. Arthur and R. Phillips (eds) *Issues in the Teaching of History*. London: Routledge.

Strong, R. (1987) *Glorianna, The Portraits of Queen Elizabeth*. London: Thames and Hudson.

Sukhnandan, L., Lee, B. and Kelleher, S. (2000) *An Investigation into Gender Differences in Achievement*. Slough: NFER.

Sutcliffe, R. (1974) *The Changeling*. London: Hamish Hamilton.

Sylvester, D. (1989) 'Children as Historians', in J. Campbell and V. Little (eds) *Humanities in the Primary School*. Lewes: Falmer Press.

Testa, F. (1982) *Never Satisfied*. London: Abelord/North-South.

Thomas, E. (1993) 'Irony Age Infants', *Times Educational Supplement* 23 April: 5.

Thomas, K. (1983) *Man and the Natural World*. London: Allen Lane.

Thompson, A. (1972) 'Some Psychological Aspects of History Teaching', in W. H. Burston and C. W. Green (eds), *A Handbook for History Teachers*, 2nd edn. London: Methuen.

Thomson, E. D. (1969) *The Aims of History*. London: Thames and Hudson.

Thornton, S. J. and Vukelich, R. (1988) 'The Effects of Children's Understanding of Time Concepts or Historical Understanding', *Theory and Research in Social Education* **16**(1): 69–82.

The Times Atlas of Ancient Civilizations (1989) London: Times Books/The Times.

Tonge, N. (1993) 'Communicating History', *Teaching History* **71**: 25–9.

Torrance, E. P. (1962) *Guiding Creative Talent*. London and New York: Prentice Hall.

Torrance, E. P. (1965) *Rewarding Creative Behaviour*. London and New York: Prentice Hall.

Treece, H. (1965) *The Bronze Sword*. London: Hamish Hamilton.

UK School Museums Group Conference (1999), St John's House, Warwick CV34 4NF.

Unstead, R. J. (1964) *From Cavemen to Vikings*. London: A & C Black Ltd.

Uttley, A. (1977) *A Traveller in Time*. Harmondsworth: Puffin.

Vishram, R. (1988) *Ayars Lascars and Princes*. London: Pluto.

Von Borries, B. and Angvik, M. (eds) (1997) *Youth and History. A Comparative European Survey on Historical Consciousness and Political Attitudes Among Adolescents*. Hamburg: Korber Stlftung edition.

Vygotsky, L. S. (1962) *Thought and Language*. Edited and translated by E. Hanfmann and G. Vakar. London and New York: Wiley.

Waddell, M. and Dale, P. (1989) *Once There Were Giants*. London: Watler Books.

Wade, B. (1981) 'Assessing Pupils' Contributions in Appreciating a Poem', *Journal of Education for Teaching* **7**(1): 49.

Wallach, M. A. and Kagan, N. (1965) *Modes of Thinking in Young Children*. London:

Holt, Rinehart and Winston.

Watts, D. G. (1972) *The Learning of History.* London: Routledge and Kegan Paul.

Watts, R. and Grosvenor, I. (eds) (1995) *Crossing the Key Stages of History.* London: David Fulton Publishers.

Wedgwood, C. V. (1955) *The King's Peace 1637–1641 (The Great Rebellion).* London: Collins.

Wedgwood, C. V. (1958) *The King's War 1641–1647.* London: Collins.

Werner, H. and Kaplan, E. (1963) *Symbol Formation, an Orgasmic Developmental Approach to Language and Expression of Thought.* London and New York: Wiley.

West, J. (1981) 'Children's Awareness of the Past'. Unpubl. Ph.D. Thesis. University of Keele.

Westall, R. (1975) *The Machine-Gunners.* London: MacMillan.

Wood, D. and Middleton, D. (1975) 'A Study of Assisted Problem-Solving', *British Journal of Psychology* **66**: 181–91.

Wood, L. and Holden, C. (1995) *Teaching Early Years History.* Cambridge: Chris Kingston Publishing.

Wray, D. (1997) *Extending Literacy: children reading and writing non-fiction.* London: Routledge.

Wray, D and Medwell, J. (1998) *Teaching English in Primary Schools: A Handbook of Teaching Strategies and Key Ideas in Literacy.* London: Letts Educational.

Wright, D. (1984) 'A Small Local Investigation', *Teaching History* **39**: 3–4.

Wright, M. (1992) *A Really Practical Guide to Primary History.* Cheltenham: Stanley Thornes.

Resources Referred to in the Text

Anglia Multimedia, Anglia House, Norwich, NR1 3JG.

The Association for the Study of African, Caribbean and Asian Culture in Britain, c/o ICS, 27-28 Russell Square, London, WC1

BBC Broadcasting Support Services, PO Box 7, London, W3 6XJ.

Benin: pictures from an African Kingdom (1992), British Museum Education Service, Great Russell Street, London, WC1.

Benin Source Pack for Key Stage 2 (1992), Northamptonshire Black History Group, from Wellingborough REC, Victorian Centre, Park Road, Wellingborough, Northants, NN8 1HT.

British Museum Education Service, Great Russell Street, London, WC1.

English Heritage Education Service, Keysign House, 429 Oxford Street, London.

Eureka Benin: An African Kingdom; video, teacher's resource booklet, poster; Educational Television Co., PO Box 100, Warwick, CV34 6TZ.

History of Advertising Trust, Norwich NR14 6NU (www.hatads.org.uk).

History in Evidence, Monk Road, Alfreson, Derbyshire.

The National Trust, 36 Queen Anne's Gate, London, SW1

Two-Can, 343 Old Street, London EC1 V9Q.

School Museums Group, St John's House, Warwick CV34 4NF.

Victorians, Music from the Past, text and audiotape (Longmans 1987)

Women's History Network, Key Stage 1, Biography Project, Department of History, University of York

Index